Praise for this and other work by Edward Einhorn

Fairy Tales of the Absurd

"The laughter feels like spring in *Fairy Tales of the Absurd*...a bright production with witty music and puppets galore....Almost unbearably funny. [Peter B. Brown's] pacing and diction are perfect."
The New York Times

"A winning cast...As director, Einhorn demonstrates a perfection of timing and expression...the gift of Einhorn is the common humanity he injects into his delightfully idiosyncratic characters."
New York Arts Magazine

"A very enjoyable show, fabulous for the adults and fabulous for the the kids."
Hi! Drama

Golem Stories

"*Golem Stories*' skillful direction, enthusiastic young cast, and fresh approach to the well-known story of the Golem of Prague give the play an energy and excitement that many larger scale productions don't have... In it simplicity and directness, *Golem Stories* is a reminder of the supernatural quality of the theater, which can transform the most basic elements of speech and play into something magical."
The Jewish Standard

"It really is quite wonderful."
Hi! Drama

"Rather than simply retell the legend of the Golem, Edward Einhorn has skillfully woven the original into yet a new cautionary tale; In sum: our words are more powerful than we imagine."
Artzine

"Edward Einhorn has skillfully written a fairy tale and love story for adults. His writing gives the players great opportunities, such as Rifka's fake mad scene which is executed with great aplomb. The style is an absurd fantasy; and as the best of the absurd genre, more than a hint of truth is borrowed from the real world."
Stage Pages

Linguish

"Edward Einhorn combines Beckett's absurd landscape with Mac Wellman's verbal Cuisinarting, and Oliver Saks' ruminations into neurodysfunctions for his oddly entertaining foray into aphasia, euphoria, and euphony."
The Village Voice

"A well-written, well-acted meeting of Kafka and Oliver Saks."
New England Review

A Shylock

"Einhorn skillfully intersperses the famed soliloquies with his own lines... [A] hard-working cast of eight romps through 24 roles. In the leads, John Blaylock plays the professor with a thoughtful performance that pulls together the disparate elements, and Catherine Dunning brings a lovely, mocking tone to the role of Hamlet."
Back Stage

Paradox in Oz

"Released to celebrate the one-hundredth anniversary of L. Frank Baum's The Wonderful Wizard of Oz, this new Oz adventure is true in its narrative style and its black-and-white artwork (by Eric Shanower) to the spirit of the beloved Oz books...both the action and the humor quotient are high, and Oz fans will read to the expected happy ending."
Booklist

"The writing is crisp and moves the episodic story along effortlessly. This is a handsome book...if your readers can't get enough of Oz, this should be on the shelves."
School Library Journal

"Edward Einhorn has captured the real spirit of the Emerald City in his *Paradox in Oz.* This gorgeous book, with a wealth of witty and archetypically Ozian illustrations by Eric Shaower, opens when a plague of aging descends on Princess Ozma's realm, forcing her to take action to save her citizens... This stefnal material is incorporated brilliantly into the Baumian weltanschauung, and Einhorn's new characters harmonize perfectly with the famous ones... This book insures that Oz will enter the new millenium in style."
Asimov's

"A satisfying synthesis of Baum's classic style and Einhorn's modern, joyfully inventive excursions into the absurd."
Arthur Kopit, author of *Nine, Indians, Wings, Y2K,* etc.

"*Paradox in Oz* does full justice to the legacy of the Oz series and will be read and re-read by children (and their parents!)."
Midwest Book Review

The Golem, Methuselah, and Shylock:

Plays by Edward Einhorn

Also by Edward Einhorn:

Paradox in Oz
The Living House of Oz

The Golem, Methuselah, and Shylock:

Plays by Edward Einhorn

Theater 61 Press

New York

Published by Theater 61 Press
A Division of Untitled Theater Company #61

Manufactured in the United States of America

Front cover photo by Edward Einhorn
Cover design and author photo by David Maxine

ISBN 0-9770197-1-3 (casebound)
ISBN 0-9770197-0-5 (paper)

Contents

To my brother David

who started it all, years ago

Introduction

Introduction

My family had a giant book of Jewish legends that I used to read as a child, whenever I was between whatever set of library books I had most recently borrowed. The book was over a thousand pages, and each time I read no more than twenty or so of them (usually at random), so I am not sure even now whether I ever read it from cover to cover. I was fascinated with all legends at the time: Jewish, Norse, Greek, Celtic, Middle Earth (Middle Earthian?), and many more. But of course, being Jewish, I connected with the Jewish legends particularly—if nothing else, I never had to return the book to the library when I was done.

Many of the stories seeped deep within my consciousness. Some of them I remembered reading in the book, but I was surprised, when researching *Golem Stories*, to find out how many stories whose origins I had forgotten came from that same volume. Those stories definitely shaped me, much as other aspects of my Jewish heritage shaped me, in ways I'm sure I still don't fully realize.

When I did reread some of the stories, I was fascinated by some, horrified by others. The stories had taught me about the world in revelatory ways, which were also ways colored by the opinions and prejudices of all the past generations. Even the blood libel, the belief that Jews use Christian children to make matzos for Passover, is a story of sorts—a story about Jews made up by those who hated them, but a story that influenced many children the way those other stories influenced me. When I wrote *Golem Stories*, I was partly writing about my reaction to all that.

I didn't realize till later that two earlier plays of mine had also been inspired by those legends. *The Living Methuselah* started out by using Methuselah as a character simply because he was long lived. I threw in Serach because I had some vague memory of wondering why she was singled out among all of Jacob's granddaughters—the Torah mentions fifty-three grandsons, but only one granddaughter. It was only after I had written her in that I discovered (or, more likely, rediscovered) there were Jewish stories about her that called her the oldest living woman in the Torah.

A Shylock is of course about a legend not created by Jews, but one that has crept into Jewish consciousness as perhaps the most frequently performed Jewish character on stage. In some ways, it has been a story that proclaims a Jew's humanity, in others a story as damaging as the blood libel. Yet one Jewish legend inspired others, so I made up the character of Jacob Levy.

One-Eyed Moses and the Churning Red Sea was made up for Untitled Theater's 24/7 Festival, in which a play had to be written overnight, rehearsed all the next day, and performed that evening. The play was written for a night themed around Jewish legends. All the plays that night had to follow a list of rules, one of which was there had to be a pirate (or someone with a hook) in the play. I think you can figure out how those factors resulted in this particular one-act concoction.

Are these plays only for Jews? I hope not, any more than ancient Greek legends are only for ancient Greeks (or legends from Middle Earth are only for, well, hobbits and such). But they definitely have a Jewish flavor, not only in the characters. One bit of that flavor is that they question the very legends they were based upon.

I have provided an appendix which gives some brief facts about the characters in the various plays, if you are interested in that sort of thing. But if you are not, feel free to read the plays and enjoy them on their own. I wrote them to make people think, but also, I wrote them to make people laugh.

Jews like to laugh.

Golem Stories

Original Productions

Golem Stories was presented by FHB Productions and Untitled Theater Company #61 at Chashama in New York City in October 2003. It was part of the Spotlight On Halloween Festival. It was directed by Glory Sims Bowen. Original music was by William Sullivan Niederkorn. Sets were by Cemre Durosoy, assisted by Susan Pislak, lighting by Aaron Mason, sound by Christopher Brooks, and puppets by Berit Johnson. Renee Hollenback was the stage manager; Jennifer Spinello was the assistant stage manager; and Caroline Costa was the assistant director. The cast was as follows:

DEVORAH .... Diana Cherkas
RIVKA .... Morgan Dover-Pearl
REBBETSIN .... Lela Frechette
RUDOLF II .... Harry Klein
MAHARAL .... Jerry Mond
JOSEPH/GOLEM .... Chris Rummel
THADDEUS .... Michael Whitney
MOSHE .... Maxwell Zener
PUPPETEERS: Christopher Betz, Talaura Harms, Molly Light, Elizabeth Anne Wood

NOTE: The director utilized black light puppetry as an aspect of this production.

Golem Stories was previously presented by FHB Productions at Chashama in New York City in March 2003. It was part of the Spotlight On Winter Festival. It was directed by Glory Sims Bowen. Sets were by Nicole Frankel, costumes by Michael Piatkowski, assisted by Yvonne Roen, lighting by Aaron Mason, and sound by Christopher Brooks. Karene Morris was the stage manager, and Lauren Popper was the assistant director. The cast was as follows:

MAHARAL .... Ian Fleet
JOSEPH/GOLEM .... Brian Glaser
REBBETSIN .... Hanna Hayes
ISAAC .... Ben Hindell
RUDOLF II .... Harry Klein
DEVORAH .... Yvonne Roen
RIVKA .... Gina Stec
THADDEUS .... Michael Whitney
MOSHE .... Maxwell Zener

NOTE: In the original script of Golem Stories *there was an extra character, Isaac, who is only referred to in the current script.*

Awards

The two shows received the following awards from the Spotlight On Festival (Spotties):

Best Play (Playwright's Award): Edward Einhorn
Best Actress: Lela Frechette
Best Featured Actor: Michael Whitney
Best Cameo: The Puppeteers (Christopher Betz, Talaura Harms, Molly Light, and Elizabeth Anne Wood)
Best Scenic Design: Cemre Durusoy, Nicole Frankel
Best Sound Design: William Niederkorn and Christopher Brooks
Best Special Effects, Technical Achievement: Berit Johnson

Golem Stories

Scene One

It is 1590, in the city of Prague. The set is a room in the home of RABBI JUDAH LOEW (the MAHARAL). It serves both as a living room and as a dining room. The furnishings are poor, despite the reputation of the Rabbi. RIVKA is sitting with JOSEPH when the curtain rises. They are playing a game, seeing how close they can come to touching without doing so. RIVKA giggles. The REBBETSIN enters. As she talks, JOSEPH and RIVKA continue to surreptitiously play their game, until the REBBETSIN's story distracts JOSEPH.

REBBETSIN: So. Where was I?

RIVKA: The idols.

REBBETSIN: Right. So Abraham took his staff and smashed all the idols in his father's store, except for the largest one. In that idol's hands, Abraham placed the staff. When Abraham's father came home, he was horrified. "Why have you done this to my business?" his father cried. And Abraham said to him, "I didn't do it, the big idol did. While you were gone, all the idols had an argument, and the big one smashed all the smaller ones." "Don't be ridiculous," said Abraham's father, "he couldn't have done that, he's nothing but a statue." "Exactly," said Abraham.

(Slight pause)

JOSEPH: Leaving his father with a store full of smashed statues.

REBBETSIN: That's not the point.

JOSEPH: But it's true. It was his father's business. How was he to know that his son had suddenly decided that there's one God, and that it was unholy to worship idols?

REBBETSIN: He hadn't just decided it. God had spoken to him.

JOSEPH: Yes, I know, but Abraham's father didn't know that. Why destroy someone's business, just because of religious differences?

REBBETSIN: I see. You think this is like your bakery.

JOSEPH: Maybe. Yes.

REBBETSIN: That was different. That was done out of hatred, pure and simple.

JOSEPH: Was it? They truly believed they had God on their side.

REBBETSIN: I'm sorry. I shouldn't have started telling you my stories. It calms me sometimes, when I'm worried. I'm afraid I'm incapable of being quiet, when I'm nervous. But I'm being selfish. Why don't I check on Devorah, see if she's ready. She's been getting ready for hour, now. It's not often we meet a king, in any circumstances. Are you ready Rivka?

RIVKA: I want to stay here, with Joseph.

REBBETISIN: Well—yes, for a moment. Your father should be back in a moment, anyway. We're all so glad you weren't hurt, Joseph. You know that. Don't worry, King Rudolf's a good man. He doesn't know much about Judaism, but he likes Judah. I think he'll do what he can.

JOSEPH: I'm sure he will.

(The REBBETSIN exits.)

RIVKA: Don't mind Mamma and her stories. She loves you, that's why she tells you those stories.

JOSEPH: I know. It's sweet. I'm sorry I was so irritable with her.

RIVKA: I think it's amazing that you haven't been more upset, considering what you've been through.

JOSEPH: We've all had hard times. I'm just lucky, because I'm engaged to the Rabbi's daughter, and he's a friend of the King. The King's actually coming here. I can't believe it, still. He must not want anyone to know he's coming, or he would have invited us to the palace.

RIVKA: *(Playfully)* Kiss me, Joseph.

JOSEPH: Kiss you?

RIVKA: Yes.

JOSEPH: We can't. I mean...it's bad enough that we've touched. By mistake. Mostly.

RIVKA: We'll be married soon. What does it matter?

JOSEPH: Then we don't have long to wait.

RIVKA: I liked it when we touched.

JOSEPH: So did I. You know that. But it's against Jewish law. What would your father think?

RIVKA: If I don't care what he thinks, why should you?

JOSEPH: He's the Maharal.

RIVKA: Joseph, I love you. And I'm scared.

JOSEPH: Scared of what?

RIVKA: Kiss me. Please.

(JOSEPH hesitates, looking at her. The MAHARAL enters.)

MAHARAL: What are you two doing? Where's your mother?

RIVKA: She's helping Devorah get ready.

MAHARAL: Still? He'll be here any minute. Why don't you go and check on them Rivka.

(RIVKA looks at JOSEPH.)

JOSEPH: Go on, Rivka. Don't worry.

(RIVKA exits.)

MAHARAL: Now, Joseph, I just want you to tell the King the truth, tonight. Don't be too afraid of him. He's come to hear our story, after all.

JOSEPH: Yes, Rabbi.

MAHARAL: Have there been any other incidents, in the last couple of days?

JOSEPH: Just a stone or two, that's all.

MAHARAL: Even that's too much.

JOSEPH: It's no more than usual. Even in good times, you can expect a stone or two.

MAHARAL: Well, that's going to change.

(The REBBETSIN enters with RIVKA and DEVORAH. They are dressed for company. Everybody but DEVORAH has a yellow circle sewn on the left arm or chest area of their clothes. The yellow circle is a required item for all Jews in Prague.)

Wonderful. You all look beautiful.

DEVORAH: Thank you. I just finished sewing this, Pappa. Do you think the King will like it?

MAHARAL: Where's your badge?

DEVORAH: I haven't sewn it on yet.

MAHARAL: Then throw on your cloak. You don't want the King to see you without a badge.

DEVORAH: My cloak? But that will look—

(There is a crash.)

What's that?

JOSEPH: It sounded like a stone.

MAHARAL: At my house?

JOSEPH: I think so. It sounds like it. And I've heard that sound often enough, recently, believe me. Do you want me to clean things up?

REBBETSIN: I'll go with you.

MAHARAL: If it's a stone, bring it here. It will be something else to show the King.

(The REBBETSIN and JOSEPH exit.)

DEVORAH: What a time for this to happen.

MAHARAL: It's a good time for this to happen. A hidden blessing. So the King knows I'm serious when I tell him about Joseph's troubles.

DEVORAH: What's he like, the King?

MAHARAL: Different. He's obsessed by mystical knowledge. That's why he likes me, I think, because he wants to learn about the Kabala. But he's an independent thinker, and that makes him good for the Jews.

RIVKA: He still makes us wear these badges.

MAHARAL: Even so. And you should put yours on, Devorah.

(The REBBETSIN and JOSEPH enter, with a stone.)

REBBETSIN: It was a stone, just as Joseph guessed.

RIVKA: Are you all right?

REBBETSIN: I'm fine. They had already run off, as usual.

DEVORAH: They're such cowards.

MAHARAL: Leave the stone on the table.

(There is a knock.)

That must be him.

JOSEPH: Or someone with another stone.

REBBETSIN: He's early.

MAHARAL: A little. It's him. The cloak, Devorah.

DEVORAH: Yes, Pappa.

(DEVORAH puts on her cloak. Everyone stands and waits tensely. Pause. The MAHARAL opens the door. RUDOLF enters, holding a cross before him. He is hidden inside a large dark cloak, which covers up his royal vestments.)

MAHARAL: Hello, your majesty. It's good to see you.

RUDOLF: It's good to see you, too, Judah.

(The MAHARAL stares at the cross.)

It's just a precaution, Judah. I hope you don't mind.

MAHARAL: I didn't know you had become so religious. You told me you were more interested in alchemy than Christianity.

RUDOLF: I am, but a learned priest told me this particular cross has special powers. It was touched by St. Paul himself. It wards off evil spirits. He advised me to use it when—when I'm in someplace unfamiliar.

MAHARAL: I assure you, I am acquainted with the full Kabala. There are no evil spirits in my house. You can feel free to put the cross down.

RUDOLF: Yes, of course.

(RUDOLF lowers the cross. JOSEPH takes his cloak.)

MAHARAL: Let me introduce you to my family. This is my wife Pearla, and these are two of my daughters, Devorah and Rivka, my youngest. And this young man is Joseph. He is Rivka's fiancé, and he's studied with me since he was very young.

RUDOLF: Is he the rabbinical student I met?

MAHARAL: No. That was Isaac, Devorah's fiancé. He's in Poland now, studying. Joseph's the baker.

RUDOLF: Where are your other daughters?

MAHARAL: Married, I'm afraid. Now that these last two are spoken for, I'm afraid you'll have to find your heir another princess.

(RUDOLF laughs, a little uncomfortably.)

RUDOLF: Well. We have some things to discuss.

MAHARAL: Perhaps you should take the girls into the kitchen while we talk.

REBBETSIN: Of course.

(The REBBETSIN, RIVKA and DEVORAH exit.)

MAHARAL: Please, sit down.

(RUDOLF sits. After he sits, so does everyone else.)

RUDOLF: Your house seems a little small.

MAHARAL: It's no smaller than it ever was. It is enough for us.

RUDOLF: I had heard that it had become bigger. As big as my palace, almost.

MAHARAL: As big as your palace? How would I ever manage that?

RUDOLF: They say some of your people stole from the treasuries.

MAHARAL: Your majesty, I assure you. We did no such thing.

RUDOLF: Well. I thought so. It didn't sound that believable a story, to me. Someone trying to save his own skin, more likely. I'm sorry I even brought it up.

MAHARAL: You'll find that a lot of the stories you've heard about us are untrue.

RUDOLF: Yes. Of course. It's just that your people are so... Why is that stone on your table? Is it religious?

MAHARAL: On the contrary. It just arrived in our house, a few minutes before you did. It was thrown through our window.

RUDOLF: Because of me?

MAHARAL: I assume that it's because Passover is coming up, next month. This sort of thing happens every year, although it's particularly bad this year.

RUDOLF: Which is why you asked me here, tonight.

MAHARAL: That's right.

RUDOLF: I don't know what I can do for you, Judah. I can't control public opinion.

MAHARAL: Perhaps not, but you could make more of an effort to find the people who throw these rocks, or worse. I rarely see an officer in this quarter, and when I do, he is usually turning a blind eye to these attacks, or even participating.

RUDOLF: Most of the guards don't want to come to this section. They're afraid of you.

MAHARAL: We've done nothing to harm them.

RUDOLF: Well, perhaps not, but some of them have children.

MAHARAL: So?

RUDOLF: They know Passover's approaching. They know you'll need matzos. They just don't want you to use their children to make them.

MAHARAL: Certainly you don't actually believe that we use the blood of Christian children to make matzos?

RUDOLF: Well, I'm not saying you personally, Judah, I'm sure you've found a different way—

MAHARAL: Matzos are unleavened bread. Nothing more.

RUDOLF: Come now, I'm on your side, but you can't tell me that no Jew has ever—

MAHARAL: That's what I'm telling you.

RUDOLF: Then why is it so widely believed?

MAHARAL: Your majesty, I'm surprised at you. Just because something is widely believed, it doesn't make it true. As a student of the sciences, you should know that more than anyone.

RUDOLF: There were always a lot of things about your religion I never understood. But that you might want to use the blood of Christian children, in revenge for what has been done to you, that made sense.

MAHARAL: Not to us. Not to any human, I hope. Eating children? Did you really believe we do that?

RUDOLF: I've heard that you spirit them away, in the deep of night. You then take the heart out of the child, so that the rest can be incinerated. This heart is placed upon a glowing coal, where it is magically transformed by your rabbis.

MAHARAL: I am one of those rabbis that they speak about, I'm sure. Do you think I transform the hearts of children?

RUDOLF: It is just a legend I have heard.

MAHARAL: Legends like that need to be questioned, because if they are not, they shape the mind of the listener into a hateful form. Even the Holy One, Blessed be He, should be questioned, if he says something that sounds immoral. That is why Abraham could plead with him to save Sodom.

RUDOLF: I don't know much about the Bible. All I know are the tales I have been told.

MAHARAL: And who told you that story?

RUDOLF: Many people. A highly respected young Jesuit priest, for one.

MAHARAL: Thaddeus?

RUDOLF: Well, yes.

MAHARAL: Thaddeus has been spreading that lie for years now. He hates us, your majesty. He would say anything to destroy us. He is the one who always incites the crowds against us.

RUDOLF: He is not the only one who's told me this story. Some of my alchemists have told me so as well, and they are experts on such transformations.

JOSEPH: I assure you, your majesty, I worked in a bakery, and never have we done anything so barbaric.

RUDOLF: I heard that they found the body of a child in your bakery.

JOSEPH: Yes, that's true.

RUDOLF: How did it get there?

JOSEPH: I don't know, your majesty. I just came in to open the shop, that morning. We take turns opening the shop, and it was just chance that it was my turn that day. When I arrived, there was a crowd already surrounding my shop, a Christian crowd, led by that priest, Thaddeus, although we almost never see Christians in this quarter. When I got to the door the child had already been placed on the doorstep. It was in a little bundle, turned dark brown with blood. I could barely look at it. Before I knew what was happening, the crowd was screaming at me, calling me a murderer and throwing stones. They burned the bakery to the ground. But the bakery was just the beginning. Since then, there have been crowds outside my door, throwing rocks and yelling curses. I live alone, thank God, so I put no one in danger but myself, but I am afraid that they will burn my home down, as well. I came to the Rabbi for help. I don't know how to prove it, your majesty, but I did not kill that child.

MAHARAL: I assure you, your majesty, that Joseph is one of the gentlest people I know. He is incapable of killing.

RUDOLF: It is hard to know what a man is truly capable of.

MAHARAL: I ask you, does it make sense that a crowd would have gathered, spontaneously, at dawn? Does it make sense that someone would commit such a terrible crime, and then leave the child on his doorstep, for all to see? Someone put that child there, horrible as it may seem to you. Then he gathered all those people, or told Thaddeus, and they marched to the bakery. Maybe it was the killer himself who spread the story.

JOSEPH: This sort of thing has happened before, your majesty. A few years ago, Thaddeus accused Jacob ben Avram of killing a young girl. Fortunately, she was found before they hanged Jacob.

MAHARAL: And in those days, he wouldn't have even gone to trial. It was before you had passed the law granting Jews the same trials Christians have.

RUDOLF: There are some people who tell me they want to hang you, Joseph.

JOSEPH: I know, your majesty.

RUDOLF: I've refused, out of friendship to Judah, and because I don't want to allow summary hangings of Jews anymore. But unless another killer is found, it will be difficult to stop the accusations against you.

JOSEPH: All I can tell you, your majesty, is that I am innocent.

RUDOLF: Well. I will do what I can.

MAHARAL: It would be helpful if you were to declare that matzos are made of flour and water, nothing more.

RUDOLF: And you swear to me this is true?

MAHARAL: I cannot swear. It is against my religious beliefs. But believe me, it's true.

RUDOLF: Hmmm. Well, as I said, affairs of state. I must be going.

(RUDOLF stands, and JOSEPH hurries to get his cloak.)

MAHARAL: I appreciate your coming to see us, your majesty.

RUDOLF: Yes. Well then, goodbye.

(RUDOLF hurries out, covering himself with his cloak so as to be unnoticed outside.)

JOSEPH: Do you think this talk did any good, Rabbi?

MAHARAL: We'll see. He seems to be a little too influenced by Thaddeus and his like, right now, for me to feel comfortable. Well, we can only hope for his goodwill. He has been good to us, so far. Tell me if anything else happens, Joseph.

JOSEPH: I will. I promise.

Scene Two

There are noises of a riot outside. Inside, DEVORAH anxiously stares out the window, while the REBBETSIN and RIVKA sit together at the table.

REBBETSIN: ...When the attack came the next night, they were prepared. The Golem stood tall above the heads of the villagers, and arrows couldn't hurt him, nor could swords. The Golem stepped forward, and with one swipe of his hand he knocked lifeless three of the attackers. Then he swiped again—

DEVORAH: Mamma, quiet, please. I just can't listen to any more stories.

REBBETSIN: I'm sorry. But it seemed to be calming Rivka. Rivka, are you feeling any better now?

RIVKA: *(Shakes her head)* He's dead.

REBBETSIN: Hush. Don't say that.

RIVKA: He's dead. I felt it. Joseph's dead.

REBBETSIN: We're all worried, darling. Your father is out there too, risking his life. But they've survived worse than this.

RIVKA: No. I know. Joseph and I have a bond. I know.

(The noise lessens.)

DEVORAH: The noise is getting less.

REBBETSIN: Does that mean it's over?

DEVORAH: The rioting is. For now. But I can't see anything. Just those fires. I hope nobody was inside those stores when they were burned.

REBBETSIN: Please God, bring us back our loved ones.

RIVKA: It's too late. It's too late for Joseph.

DEVORAH: I see someone, I think, through the smoke. He's coming here.

REBBETSIN: It that good or bad?

DEVORAH: It's Moshe.

REBBETSIN: Moshe? Just Moshe?

RIVKA: You see? Joseph isn't with him. It's what I thought. It's what I thought.

REBBETSIN: Hush. Your father and Joseph will be coming soon, too.

DEVORAH: It's not just you who's worried, Rivka. But you've got to try to stay calm.

RIVKA: I am calm. The hysteria is over. Now I'm nothing but calm.

REBBETSIN: Moshe will bring news. Don't worry, Rivka.

DEVORAH: Here he is.

(MOSHE opens the door.)

REBBETSIN: Moshe, I'm glad to see you're all right. How's—

RIVKA: He's dead, isn't he?

DEVORAH: She means Joseph. She's been so worried.

MOSHE: I'm sorry, Rivka.

REBBETSIN: You don't mean?

MOSHE: Yes. Joseph's dead.

(RIVKA gasps.)

DEVORAH: Rivka! I'm sorry. Do you...do you want some water?

RIVKA: No, I don't want *water*. Just leave me alone.

(RIVKA exits.)

REBBETSIN: Why don't you get Moshe water, Devorah. I'm sure he's thirsty.

MOSHE: Yes, I am. A bit.

(DEVORAH exits.)

REBBETSIN: Did you see my husband, Moshe?

MOSHE: I lost sight of him. But I'm sure he's all right. The last time I saw him, he was unhurt.

REBBETSIN: When did you lose sight of him?

MOSHE: A few hours ago.

REBBETSIN: Hours. I see.

(DEVORAH enters, with water.)

REBBETSIN: How did Joseph...?

MOSHE: A stone. Just well placed, this time.
DEVORAH: Oh. Poor Joseph.
REBBETSIN: My poor Rivka.
DEVORAH: I thought the King...
MOSHE: He can stop a hanging. But no one can stop a mob. At least, not one led by Thaddeus.
DEVORAH: Thaddeus again.
MOSHE: Yes.
(There is a knock on the door. Everyone freezes.)
Who is it?
MAHARAL (OS): It's me.
MOSHE: Rabbi?
REBBETSIN: Judah!
MAHARAL (OS): Yes. Moshe, I need your help.
(MOSHE opens the door. The MAHARAL drags in a body. It is the GOLEM. The GOLEM should be played by the actor playing JOSEPH, though as the GOLEM his skin should be colored gray and he shouldn't have a beard [or possibly any hair]. DEVORAH stifles a scream.)
REBBETSIN: Judah, what are you doing?
MAHARAL: This is not what it seems to be.
REBBETSIN: What is it then?
MAHARAL: This is a golem.
REBBETSIN: A golem? A real golem?
MAHARAL: I believe so.
DEVORAH: But it looks like...
MAHARAL: Joseph. Yes, I know.
REBBETSIN: But...how?
MAHARAL: I had a dream, before the attack had begun. It told me to go down to the riverside and fashion the likeness of a man out of the loam I found on the banks. During the battle, I realized what the dream was telling me. And so I left, and for hours I built this creature. You've read the stories about golems in the past, those great creatures of clay that have been built to help us in times such as these.

Well, God has led me to build one for us this time, for our protection.

DEVORAH: But why does it look like Joseph?

MAHARAL: Golems are half demon, but they must also join with a human soul. After I had built this creature, it suddenly transformed into the likeness of Joseph. I didn't know why, at first. Then I heard that he had died.

REBBETSIN: Yes.

MOSHE: Then, um…has this creature stolen Joseph's soul?

MAHARAL: No. Joseph's soul joined with it, so that he could help protect us, as he tried to when he was alive.

DEVORAH: And then...what? What happens to it, now?

MAHARAL: Now, I must awaken the Golem.

MOSHE: Are you sure it's safe? I've heard that they can go a little out of control.

MAHARAL: That was only when they were maltreated. We must be careful, it's true, and treat him well. But we need him. You saw what happened tonight. We can't sit around and be slaughtered like lambs. We must defend ourselves. And I will need your help to bring him to life, Moshe.

MOSHE: My help? I don't know much about the Kabala, Rabbi. And these things…make me uneasy.

MAHARAL: You know a lot about the Torah. You don't need to know much more. I will need all three of you. Devorah and Pearla, too. Two men and two women, that's perfect.

DEVORAH: Will he still look like Joseph, when he is awake?

MAHARAL: Even more so, I suspect.

REBBETSIN: Where will he stay?

MAHARAL: With us. With our family.

REBBETSIN: That will be very hard on Rivka.

MAHARAL: I know. I'm sorry, but we don't have much choice.

MOSHE: What do we need to do?

MAHARAL: Move him to the center of the room, first, so I can cast a circle around him.

(MOSHE does, and the MAHARAL draws a chalk circle.)

MOSHE: He feels so alive. So human. If I hadn't seen Joseph earlier tonight...

MAHARAL: I know. But it's important to remember that he's not human. Even when he is alive, he'll be half demon. This is not your friend from the Yeshiva, Moshe. This is a force of God, made life. Don't forget it, any of you.

DEVORAH: I'm not likely to.

REBBETSIN: What do we need to do now, Judah?

MAHARAL: We must stand at the Golem's feet. Each of us is supposed to represent an element. I know I was born under the element of Air and Pearla was born under the element of Fire. You were born under the element of Water, weren't you, Devorah?

DEVORAH: Yes.

MOSHE: So was I.

MAHARAL: That's all right. The Golem itself can be the representative of Earth. Now I will need my siddur. What's happened to it?

DEVORAH: It's over there, Pappa. I saw Rivka reading it.

MAHARAL: She shouldn't have been. None of you should. Not this siddur. I've told her that.

DEVORAH: I know, Pappa.

MAHARAL: Now, I will need Pearla and Devorah to circle the Golem seven times, while I chant the 61-syllable name of God that belongs under the Sephira Tepheret and the 99-syllable name of God that belongs under the Sephira Netzoch. Moshe, I want you to hold down its legs and pray along with me. Make sure it doesn't rise, until I command it. I can do the rest.

(The MAHARAL places the two lanterns on either side of the GOLEM while the REBBETSIN and DEVORAH stand at his feet.)

Very well. Begin.

(DEVORAH and the REBBETSIN circle, and the MAHARAL speaks in Hebrew syllables. It should sound musical, like a chant.

There should be some suggestion of a fire, either aurally or visually, then a suggestion of water. Finally, they finish circling, and the MAHARAL takes his place at the foot of the GOLEM. There is a suggestion of wind.)

MAHARAL: As it is said in the book of Genesis, "And he breathed the spirit of life into his nostrils, and man became a living creature." As I write the word *Emet* upon your forehead, which means truth, God will breathe the spirit of life into you.

(The light flares bright white for a second, then dims to its original color. The GOLEM takes one convulsive breath, then breathes normally, if somewhat laboriously.)

Rise to your feet!

(The GOLEM totters to his feet.)

Know that we have created you from the clay so that you might be the defender of the Jewish people, guarding them against all enemies. You will be possessed of great strength, great enough to crush a rock with your bare hands, great enough to crush an enemy before you. You will be called Joseph Golem, after the man whose soul you carry. You will live with me here, and you will do all I request until it is done in its entirety. Do you understand?

(The GOLEM nods his head.)

Good.

DEVORAH: Why doesn't he speak?

MAHARAL: I have given him the power to move and to hear and to sense, but only God can give the power to speak.

REBBETSIN: What are you going to have him do?

MAHARAL: For now, I will have him work only as our servant. We will say he is our mute cousin, come to stay with us for a while. Then, when there are more attacks, we will have him ready to defend us.

REBBETSIN: Is it safe to keep him in our house?

MAHARAL: He is bound to us. He will listen only to our orders. It is safe.

(RIVKA enters.)

RIVKA: Is everyone—Joseph!

REBBETSIN: No, Rivka, don't look.

(The GOLEM puts out his hand, and takes a step towards RIVKA.)

MAHARAL: Joseph, stop!

(The GOLEM freezes in place. The REBBETSIN grabs RIVKA and hugs her, while holding her back.)

REBBETSIN: Don't look, Rivka, don't look.

(The GOLEM and RIVKA stare at each other. Blackout.)

Scene Three

It is evening, the next day. DEVORAH is comforting RIVKA. The table is half set.

DEVORAH: You should lie down, Rivka. You were up all night. Try to get an hour of sleep, at least, before dinner.

RIVKA: I just feel that somehow, if I had told Joseph to stay here, with us, he wouldn't have been killed. If only I had it to live over again. We knew, we knew that they had been throwing stones at him. What did we expect, that just because the King had visited us, they would stop?

DEVORAH: We couldn't have known. No one could have known.

RIVKA: Of course we could have. How many others have died, just like he has, over the last ten years? Benjamin, Reuben, Eliyahu. Even Bezalel. All dead. And now Joseph. Why? What makes them want to kill us so much?

DEVORAH: They think that we're all witches and demons.

RIVKA: They're the demons. They are.

DEVORAH: Please, Rivka, just try to get some rest. Just try.

RIVKA: How can I sleep?

DEVORAH: I don't know. But you need to try, at least. Please. I'll take you to bed.

(The GOLEM enters, silently, with candlesticks.)

RIVKA: I wish...I wish...

DEVORAH: What do you wish, Rivka?

RIVKA: I wish I could see him. Just one last time. Tell him I love him, at least.

DEVORAH: Oh. I'm sure he knew that.

RIVKA: I just wish I could tell him.

(RIVKA turns and sees the GOLEM and screams.)

RIVKA: How long have you been here? How long have you been listening?

DEVORAH: Shhh. He can't answer you. He can't speak.

(The REBBETSIN comes running in.)

REBBETSIN: Is everything all right? What happened?

DEVORAH: What's he doing here? He scared us half to death.

REBBETSIN: I'm sorry. I asked him to put the candlesticks out. He's helping to set the table.

DEVORAH: Well then, what's he just standing there, for?

REBBETSIN: Put the candlesticks on the table, Joseph.

RIVKA: Don't call him that.

(She runs from the room. The GOLEM puts the candlesticks on the table.)

REBBETSIN: I don't know what to call him. Joseph is his name.

DEVORAH: Just call him Golem.

REBBETSIN: That's not a name.

DEVORAH: He responds to it. Look. Sit down, Golem.

(The GOLEM sits down.)

Stand up, Golem.

(The GOLEM stands up.)

Jump up and down Golem.

(The GOLEM jumps. DEVORAH laughs.)

Actually, this could be kind of fun. Run in place, Golem.

(The GOLEM runs in place.)

REBBETSIN: Devorah, stop that. Why don't you go and change for dinner? I'll finish setting the table.

DEVORAH: Are you sure you should be alone with him?

REBBETSIN: I'll be fine. Go.

(DEVORAH exits.)

I'm sorry about that, Joseph. Golem.

(The GOLEM keeps running.)

You can stop running. Why don't you sit down, while I set the table?

(The GOLEM sits.)

REBBETSIN: That's better, isn't it? I would like you to avoid Rivka, if you could, for a while at least. I know it's a small house, but she misses Joseph so much. *(The REBBETSIN sits down.)* You really do look like Joseph. It's hard to believe you're half demon. And it's hard to believe that you're going to fight anyone, sitting here with you. You look so—so harmless. I mean that well. The world needs more harmless people. *(The REBBETSIN stands up and continues to set the table.)* I know an old story about some demons. Well, witches really. Do you mind if I tell it to you? It would make me feel—I don't know, maybe as if things weren't so horrible. I always used to tell the children stories while I was setting the table or going through the synagogue accounts. I used to tell stories to Joseph, too, when I helped him with the bakery accounts. He seemed to like it. *(The REBBETSIN looks at the GOLEM silently, for a minute.)* Do you understand what I'm saying? *(Silence)* Anyway, I'm sorry, I was supposed to tell you a story. It happened that, in such-and-such a city, there was a cave inhabited by eighty witches. Into this city came a great Rabbi, and people came to him, and they said, "There are eighty witches in the cave nearby, and they have done this and that." So the Rabbi asked for eighty of their most stalwart men, and he gave each man a vessel, and within each vessel was a robe. And he told the men that he would whistle two times. On the first whistle, they were instructed to put on their robes. On the second, they were instructed to run in and lift the witches from the ground. And the Rabbi went with these men on a rainy day to the cave, and he told them to hide. Then he called out to the witches, "Let me in, for I am one of you." And they asked, "Why have you come?" And he said, "To teach and to learn." So the witches let him in, and they showed him many pleasures. And they asked him, "What can you show us?" And he said, "I can whistle once, and there will appear eighty young men, who will make merry with you." And he whistled once, and the men appeared. And their robes were dry, even though outside it was raining, because they had kept them in their vessels. So the witches became very impressed with the power of the Rabbi. And the Rabbi said,

"Let each one choose his partner." And he whistled again, and each man raised up a witch from the ground, which deprived them of their powers. And the witches were taken into town, where they were hanged. And this is how the Rabbi outwitted the eighty witches.

GOLEM: How did the Rabbi know they were really witches?

REBBETSIN: What? *(The GOLEM is silent and still.)* Judah, come quickly! *(She looks at the GOLEM again.)* What did you say? Did you say something? *(The GOLEM is silent.)* Joseph? Look at me. *(The GOLEM looks at her.)* Did you say something to me, just now? *(The GOLEM nods.)* Judah!

(The MAHARAL enters.)

MAHARAL: What's wrong?

REBBETSIN: The Golem just spoke.

MAHARAL: Don't be ridiculous. You must be imagining it.

REBBETSIN: I just heard him.

MAHARAL: That's impossible. Only God gives the power of speech.

GOLEM: Even if they were witches, why did they have to hang them? What's wrong with being a witch?

REBBETSIN: Did you hear him?

MAHARAL: Joseph, how did you learn this power of speech?

REBBETSIN: You said he was half demon. Maybe that's the half that's talking.

GOLEM: All they did was show him pleasures.

MAHARAL: What have you been talking to him about?

REBBETSIN: I was just telling him a story.

GOLEM: What pleasures did they show him?

MAHARAL: Joseph, stand here in front of me. I command you to tell me, is it God or your demon nature that have put these words into your mouth?

GOLEM: Neither.

MAHARAL: Then why have you spoken?

GOLEM: I was just wondering, that's all. I didn't understand the story.

MAHARAL: You don't understand my question. How did you learn to speak?

GOLEM: I don't know. How did you learn to speak?

REBBETSIN: Judah, what's wrong with him?

MAHARAL: Are you still willing to obey us in all matters?

GOLEM: Yes.

MAHARAL: Are you still here as our defender?

GOLEM: Yes.

MAHARAL: Nothing is wrong with him. God has granted him the power of speech, that's all.

REBBETSIN: Why?

MAHARAL: I don't know. But I don't think we have anything to fear from him.

REBBETSIN: I hope not.

GOLEM: Could you tell me the story again? Maybe I'll understand it more this time.

REBBETSIN: There's no time, today. Maybe I'll tell it to you again, tomorrow. It wouldn't be a good idea to talk to anyone outside of our family, however.

GOLEM: Why not?

REBBETSIN: I think they found the fact that you don't talk somehow...comforting.

Scene Four

The MAHARAL is casting a Kabalistic spell. As he casts, the REBBETSIN enters. He finishes.

REBBETSIN: Have you made the house safe?

MAHARAL: As safe as I can.

REBBETSIN: Maybe I should fetch the girls, then.

MAHARAL: No. Leave them. At least till the Golem comes back. It may be safe in here, but it's not outside. There are lots of people in the synagogue with them. It's probably a lucky thing they were working in the synagogue. It may be one of the safest places in the quarter.

REBBETSIN: Usually, I go with them. I just didn't have time, and they know enough about the accounting…

MAHARAL: They have the Golem. It will protect them.

REBBETSIN: I keep thinking of Bezalel…

MAHARAL: I know, Pearla. But this is different.

(A sound is heard from outside. The REBBETSIN jumps up in alarm.)

REBBETSIN: Who is it?

(RIVKA come running in and buries her head in her mother's arms, crying. DEVORAH follows her.)

What happened?

DEVORAH: The Golem, he…it was like he was a ghost.

REBBETSIN: A ghost?

(The GOLEM enters, wearing torn and bloody clothes.)

Joseph! I thought you said he couldn't be hurt.

MAHARAL: I didn't think he could.

REBBETSIN: Look at him. Those are Joseph's old clothes.

RIVKA: He stole them, Mamma. He stole them from Joseph.

DEVORAH: He appeared in those old clothes, and it scared all the attackers away. They thought he was a ghost. They thought he was Joseph, back from the dead.

GOLEM: I am.

(RIVKA stares at him with fear.)

RIVKA: He can speak?

MAHARAL: Yes, he can speak. We just discovered it. Why are you wearing Joseph's old clothes?

GOLEM: To scare people.

RIVKA: When did he start speaking?

MAHARAL: Recently. What do you mean by scare people?

GOLEM: I thought, if I appeared in my old clothes, people would think I was a witch. People are afraid of witches.

MAHARAL: A witch? Don't you mean a ghost?

GOLEM: No one ever told me any stories about a ghost.

RIVKA: How come you didn't tell me, Pappa?

MAHARAL: About what?

RIVKA: That he could speak.

MAHARAL: I thought I did. I told Devorah.

RIVKA: Well, you didn't.

REBBETSIN: We didn't want you to be upset.

MAHARAL: Please, Rivka, I'm trying to figure out what happened.

DEVORAH: The Golem appeared from nowhere. Someone threw a rock at him, but he caught it and crushed it with his bare hands.

REBBETSIN: With his bare hands?

MAHARAL: He is supposed to be strong.

GOLEM: It wasn't hard. Anyone could have done it.

MAHARAL: Where did you get those clothes from?

GOLEM: My house.

MAHARAL: Your house?

GOLEM: Joseph's house, I mean.

MAHARAL: So you planned to do this, from the moment you left here?

GOLEM: Do what?

MAHARAL: Scare them. Make them think you were a ghost, or a witch, or whichever.

GOLEM: I made them run away.

MAHARAL: I hope they didn't think you were a witch. They already think that all Jews are witches, or at least that the women are.
DEVORAH: He also let out this terrible whine. A kind of inhuman scream.
MAHARAL: I thought we told you not to speak.
GOLEM: I wasn't speaking. I was howling. Like a dybbuk.
MAHARAL: A dybbuk?
GOLEM: They are dead spirits that possess their lovers.
DEVORAH: I think Mamma must have told him a story about them, too.
GOLEM: Yes, Mamma told me about them.
RIVKA: Don't ever call her that. Call her the Rebbetsin.
GOLEM: The Rebbetsin.
DEVORAH: I don't know why you must always tell those stories.
REBBETSIN: How was I to know he would take it so literally?
DEVORAH: Maybe it was for the best. They did run away. And nobody was killed.
MAHARAL: Not this time.

Scene Five

The REBBETSIN is sorting through papers as she tells RIVKA a story. The GOLEM stands motionless.

REBBETSIN: This is the story of the weasel and the well. There was a girl who happened to be walking to her father's house, and she became very thirsty. As there was no one with her to give her water, she climbed down into a well, and drank. But when she tried to climb up, she couldn't, so she began to weep. A man passed by and heard her. He looked down at her and asked, "Are you human, or demon?" And she said, "I am human." And he said, "Swear to me you are human." And she said, "I am human." And he said, "What happened to you?" And she said "This and that." And he said, "I will save you from the well, and then you will be mine." And she said, "Yes." And so he pulled her up. When he pulled her up, he wanted right away to take her. But she said, "What is your name?" And he told her and said, "I am from such and such a place." And she said, "I'm also from such and such a place. Come with me, and we will be married." And he said, "Who will witness this?" And she said "The weasel, and the well." And so the weasel and the well witnessed their promise, and she kept it, but he, once he left her, forgot about her and married someone else. And they had a child, but when the child was three months old, the weasel killed it. Then he had another child, but when it was three months old, it fell into the well and died.

GOLEM: The poor children.

REBBETSIN: Shhh. And his wife said, why are our children dying such peculiar deaths? And he told her, and she said, "You must follow the fate that the Holy One, Blessed be He, has given you." And so the man went to find the girl from the well, who had been feigning madness. Every time a suitor would come to her, she would laugh and dance and talk nonsense. And soon no one came, any longer. When the man came, the townspeople warned him of her madness, but he laughed, and when they met, she acted sane once more. And he said, "I accept every blemish found in you." And she said...

RIVKA: I have kept my promise.

(Pause)

GOLEM: If she had been a demon, would he have pulled her out of the well?

REBBETSIN: You listen to everything, don't you?

GOLEM: Would he have?

REBBETSIN: Well—no, probably not.

GOLEM: Why not?

REBBETSIN: He would have been afraid of her. He would have run away from her, probably.

GOLEM: Like everybody ran away from me?

REBBETSIN: Well, perhaps.

GOLEM: Would he have tried to kill her, like the witches?

REBBETSIN: No. I don't know. I think he just would have been afraid of her.

GOLEM: Why was the girl feigning madness?

REBBETSIN: So that no one else would marry her.

GOLEM: What do you mean, he wanted right away to take her?

REBBETSIN: He wanted to...marry her immediately. He didn't want to wait.

(RIVKA starts crying.)

REBBETSIN: What's wrong?

RIVKA: He looks so much like Joseph.

(RIVKA runs out.)

GOLEM: But I am Joseph.

REBBETSIN: She doesn't mean that. She was going to marry another Joseph, the man whose spirit you have. But he died, of course.

GOLEM: But I am Joseph.

REBBETSIN: You are a different Joseph.

GOLEM: She could marry me.

REBBETSIN: You are not a human being. She must marry a human being.

GOLEM: Why am I not human?

REBBETSIN: Your spirit is half demon. And you are made of clay.

GOLEM: But I am Joseph.

REBBETSIN: Her father has found her another suitor, anyway. The man who helped bring you to life, though I don't suppose you remember that. We're going to have them meet, when she's ready. It's for the best. There's so much tragedy in our community, right now, it's best not to let yourself dwell on it. I know. I remember how it was, with Bezalel.

GOLEM: Who was Bezalel?

REBBETSIN: My son. My only son. He died ten years ago, during a pogrom in Germany. They have them everywhere, you know, not just here. They set fire to a synagogue, and Bezalel happened to be in it. He loved stories, just like you did. He used to make them up. And then he died, for no reason. Like Joseph. Like so many others. I'm glad to have you here, Joseph. In a way, you remind me of my son.

GOLEM: The way I remind Rivka of Joseph?

REBBETSIN: No. It's complicated. Even I forget sometimes that you're a golem. When I see you in the corner of my eye—it's easy to believe that Joseph is alive again.

(RIVKA enters.)

RIVKA: I'm sorry I got so upset.

REBBETSIN: That's all right, dear. I understand.

GOLEM: Tell us another legend.

REBBETSIN: Perhaps that's enough, for now. I have to go stir the fire, anyway

RIVKA: No, don't worry about me. As long as it's not about marriage, I don't mind.

GOLEM: Could you tell me one, Rivka?
RIVKA: Me? Why do you want to hear a story from me?
GOLEM: You tell good stories.
RIVKA: How would you know?
REBBETSIN: It's true, dear, you do.
GOLEM: What's your favorite?
RIVKA: The one about the one, true friend.
REBBETSIN: Really? I don't remember telling you that one.
RIVKA: You didn't. I read it myself.
GOLEM: Tell it to me.
REBBETSIN: You don't have to, Rivka.

(The REBBETSIN exits to the kitchen.)

GOLEM: Please Rivka.
RIVKA: All right. Just this one story. In such and such a town, there was a philosopher who was dying. He called his son to him and asked, "How many friends do you have, in life?" "About a hundred," his son answered. "A hundred?" his father replied, " I have live so many years more than you, and I have but one true friend." So his father told him to take a pig, and slaughter it, put it in a burlap bag, and go to each of his friends and say "I have just killed a man! Bury it in your yard and no one will know. That way you can save me from hanging." So the son did what his father had told him, and each friend shut the door on him, and told him to look somewhere else for help. Then the son came back to the father, and told him what had happened. So the father said, "Go to my friend such and such, and tell him your story." The son did so, and the friend took the bag, and buried it. When he had done so, the son revealed the true contents of the bag. "I only came to prove you as a friend of my father's, and now I know what he means by a true friend," the son said.
GOLEM: And what did he mean?
RIVKA: A true friend is someone who will not abandon you, in need.

GOLEM: I see. I think that's my favorite story, too.
RIVKA: Why?
GOLEM: Because nobody died in it. Nobody but the pig.
(The REBBETSIN enters.)
REBBETSIN: I think we've had enough stories, now.
RIVKA: He really is a lot like a child.
REBBETSIN: Yes, I know.
RIVKA: How will he be able to protect us? I thought he was created to do battle.
REBBETSIN: I don't know. But your father must have known what he was doing, when he created him.
GOLEM: Who was I created to do battle with?
REBBETSIN: The people you fought recently. When you dressed up in Joseph's clothing.
GOLEM: But I didn't fight them. I arrived, and they ran away.
REBBETSIN: Next time, you may have to fight.
GOLEM: I hope not.
REBBETSIN: Why not?
GOLEM: I am not as strong as people think I am. And I don't like fighting.
REBBETSIN: Of course you're strong. You're very strong. You crushed a rock in your bare hands the other day.
GOLEM: No I didn't.
REBBETSIN: Of course you did. Everybody saw you.
GOLEM: It just looked like I did. It was a clump of dirt that looked like a rock.
REBBETSIN: But I thought—never mind. Don't worry Joseph, the Rabbi wouldn't have created you without a reason. When you are in battle, I'm sure, you will be strong enough.

Scene Six

It is the next day. The MAHARAL is reading, silently. THADDEUS enters, holding a cross before him. The MAHARAL doesn't notice him. THADDEUS mutters a prayer to himself. The MAHARAL looks up.

MAHARAL: Who are you? How did you get in here?

THADDEUS: My name is Thaddeus. I came through the front door. It was unlocked, and I did not wish to knock. I did not wish you to hide anything from me.

MAHARAL: Thaddeus.

THADDEUS: Yes.

MAHARAL: I've heard of you, of course.

THADDEUS: Of course.

MAHARAL: So you've finally decided to get rid of me, as well. I knew that Rudolf would only hold you back for so long.

THADDEUS: That's not why I've come.

MAHARAL: Then why have you come?

THADDEUS: I've come to meet him.

MAHARAL: Him?

THADDEUS: The demon.

MAHARAL: The demon?

THADDEUS: You know who I'm talking about.

MAHARAL: Yes. Yes, in fact I do.

THADDEUS: Good. I'm glad you know better than to try to lie to me.

MAHARAL: I see no reason to.

THADDEUS: Nor do I.

MAHARAL: We call him a golem. He is only half-demon.

THADDEUS: Semantics.

MAHARAL: Yes. I suppose, to you.

THADDEUS: I want to meet him.

MAHARAL: Why?

THADDEUS: I intend to destroy him.
MAHARAL: Then why should I introduce you to him?
THADDEUS: There are a group of men waiting for my order to burn down your house, if you do not.
MAHARAL: I see.
THADDEUS: If I meet him, we will leave peacefully. After I destroy him.
MAHARAL: And what if you cannot destroy him?
THADDEUS: I believe I can.
MAHARAL: I will only introduce you to him, on the understanding that you will leave peacefully, whether you destroy him or not.
THADDEUS: Don't you believe your golem will protect you?
MAHARAL: I prefer to use him only as a last resort.
THADDEUS: Very well. I agree.
MAHARAL: Swear it, upon the cross you wear about your neck.
THADDEUS: Very clever.
MAHARAL: Do it, please.
THADDEUS: I swear it, upon the cross about my neck.
MAHARAL: Good. Joseph!
THADDEUS: So, he has a name.
MAHARAL: Every creature has a name.
THADDEUS: If someone bothers to name it.
(The GOLEM enters.)
MAHARAL: Joseph, this is Thaddeus. You've heard of him. I believe you may even have met him, during that incident at the synagogue, when you pretended to be Joseph's ghost. He has come to destroy you.
THADDEUS: He does look uncannily like the baker.
MAHARAL: That is deliberate. A commentary on injustice.
THADDEUS: I see. Hello, Joseph. *(Pause)* Doesn't he speak?
MAHARAL: No.
THADDEUS: How peculiar.
MAHARAL: Do you think so?

THADDEUS: I am going to take out a cross. You may want to stand back, so as to not be singed.

MAHARAL: Another cross? If the first didn't singe me, why would the second?

THADDEUS: It is a particularly holy cross.

MAHARAL: I'll take my chances.

(THADDEUS takes out the cross.)

THADDEUS: It is over a thousand years old. It is said it was touched by St. Paul himself.

MAHARAL: I hear there a few of those going around.

THADDEUS: I am about to pray. You may want to cover your ears, for your own safety.

MAHARAL: I've heard praying before. Even Christian prayer.

THADDEUS: As you like. *(THADDEUS circles the GOLEM while he speaks an incantation.)* Most cunning serpent, you shall no more dare to deceive the human race, persecute the church, torment God's elect and sift them as wheat. The Most High God commands you, He with whom in your great insolence you still claim to be equal.

MAHARAL: It doesn't seem to be doing much good.

(THADDEUS ignores him, coming to the end, and sticking the cross against the GOLEM's forehead. Nothing happens.)

THADDEUS: Interesting. It is very powerful magic.

MAHARAL: Yes.

THADDEUS: Your own?

MAHARAL: God's.

THADDEUS: I thought we were going to be honest.

MAHARAL: I am.

THADDEUS: I see. *(THADDEUS takes out a vial of water, with which he splashes the GOLEM.)* The power of Christ compels you! The power of Christ compels you! The power of Christ compels you!

MAHARAL: Any luck?

THADDEUS: How do I know this is truly your demon?

MAHARAL: You've seen him before.

THADDEUS: He seems far too human.

MAHARAL: Not everything is what you expect it to be, Thaddeus.

THADDEUS: I suppose not.

MAHARAL: Not even the Jews.

THADDEUS: How do you know what I expect?

MAHARAL: You think we're demons, too, of sorts. But when you look close, we're surprisingly human.

THADDEUS: Appearances can be deceiving.

MAHARAL: We're real people, Thaddeus. Real women and children whom you want put to death.

THADDEUS: I did not come here to debate with you.

(He pulls out a knife. He sticks it into the GOLEM's arm. The GOLEM begins to bleed.)

This is no demon.

MAHARAL: Of course it is. I built him myself, out of clay.

(THADDEUS lifts up his arm, as if to stab the GOLEM in the heart. The GOLEM runs offstage. THADDEUS laughs.)

THADDEUS: You think he will protect you? You're deceiving yourself.

MAHARAL: I put my faith in God.

THADDEUS: That would be a good idea, if only you knew who God truly was.

MAHARAL: We each have our own beliefs.

THADDEUS: But yours are delusions. Like your belief in this golem of yours. Why don't you call him back?

MAHARAL: Joseph?

(Pause)

THADDEUS: What happened to him?

MAHARAL: I don't know.

THADDEUS: Never mind. I'm no longer interested in destroying your so-called demon, anymore. Depend on him, if you like. I think, next time, we won't have much to fear from him.

(THADDEUS exits.)

MAHARAL: Joseph!

(The GOLEM enters.)

Why didn't you come, the first time I called?

GOLEM: I didn't want him to stab me, again.

MAHARAL: But you must come when I call. He could not have hurt you, in truth.

GOLEM: It certainly seemed like he hurt me.

MAHARAL: Are you all right?

GOLEM: Yes. I don't think it's a serious injury.

MAHARAL: You had better have the Rebbetsin tend to it, nonetheless. I didn't know you could bleed.

GOLEM: I didn't know, either.

MAHARAL: Why didn't you do anything, when he attacked you?

GOLEM: I thought it would only provoke him more.

MAHARAL: Who knows, you may be right. You may be right. It may have been the wisest move, to let him believe you are no threat.

GOLEM: Am I really a threat?

MAHARAL: I hope to God you are, for our sake. You must be.

Scene Seven

The GOLEM is sitting at the table, working with clay. Beside him are ten miniature figures he's already made. He is moving them about, enacting a story.

GOLEM: There were three demons who lived in such and such a place. One day a rabbi came, and he destroyed them. *(He smashes three figures.)* No. *(He rebuilds the figures.)* They were all friends. And they did this and that. *(He dances them about, randomly.)* And then a girl came. And they wanted right away to take her. *(He pushes a fourth figure in.)* But she said, "No."

(He smashes a figure again. DEVORAH enters. She stops and watches him.)

And then a ghost came, and they ran away.

(He makes a moaning sound, and they run. He picks up one of the figures that he smashed before, and he works on it silently.)

DEVORAH: How come you can speak?

(The GOLEM is silent, engrossed in his task.)

Golem, answer me. How come you can speak?

GOLEM: I'm sorry. I didn't realize you expected an answer.

DEVORAH: So what is it? How can you speak?

GOLEM: According to your father, the gift of speech is given by God. I suppose God must have given it to me.

DEVORAH: Why?

GOLEM: I don't know.

DEVORAH: Demons are supposed to have powers, too. In many stories, they can speak. Did God give them that power?

GOLEM: I suppose.

DEVORAH: You shouldn't speak to my sister.

GOLEM: Why not?

DEVORAH: I don't have to explain myself. It's an order. I can give you any order I wish.

GOLEM: True.

(Pause. DEVORAH continues to watch him.)

I don't like your order.

DEVORAH: It doesn't matter if you like my order.

GOLEM: True. *(Pause)* Of course, if God has given me the power of speech, maybe you should not give me the opposite order.

DEVORAH: What do you know about God?

GOLEM: Very little.

DEVORAH: It upsets my sister to hear you talk. You remind her of Joseph.

GOLEM: I am Joseph.

DEVORAH: You are a demon.

GOLEM: True.

DEVORAH: Stop saying that.

GOLEM: What?

DEVORAH: True.

GOLEM: Why?

DEVORAH: Because I order it.

GOLEM: Oh.

(Pause)

DEVORAH: What are you doing?

GOLEM: Making little people.

DEVORAH: Why?

GOLEM: As presents.

DEVORAH: I saw you moving them around.

GOLEM: I was telling them a story.

DEVORAH: They are not alive. They couldn't hear you.

GOLEM: One of them is a wedding present. You're going to get married soon, aren't you?

DEVORAH: As soon as Isaac returns from Poland. You made me a present?

GOLEM: Yes.

DEVORAH: Which one?

(The GOLEM holds out a figure.)

GOLEM: This one.

(DEVORAH takes figure and looks at it.)

DEVORAH: It's me.

GOLEM: Yes.

DEVORAH: I don't know if I should accept it. It seems a little like an idol.

GOLEM: What's an idol?

DEVORAH: A statue, usually of a pagan god.

GOLEM: Are you a god?

DEVORAH: No, of course not.

GOLEM: Then I don't understand your objection.

DEVORAH: They are usually made of clay, and they look human.

GOLEM: Like me?

DEVORAH: They don't talk.

GOLEM: Maybe that's why God gave me the power of speech. So I wouldn't be an idol.

DEVORAH: Nobody worships you. It's not the same.

GOLEM: Are you going to worship your statue?

DEVORAH: No.

GOLEM: Then it shouldn't be a problem. Think of it as a little golem.

DEVORAH: God forbid. I don't want it to come alive on me.

GOLEM: Why not?

DEVORAH: Who knows what it would do.

GOLEM: Protect you, probably. I've made one for Isaac, as well.

DEVORAH: Isaac can protect himself.

(RIVKA enters.)

Remember what I said about her, Golem.

(DEVORAH exits.)

RIVKA: What did she say about me? *(Silence)* What did she say? *(Silence)* What are those things you're making? *(Silence)* Don't you speak, anymore?

GOLEM: She told me not to talk to you.

RIVKA: She what? Why?
GOLEM: She was afraid it would upset you too much.
RIVKA: Why?
GOLEM: She was afraid I would remind you of me.
RIVKA: Of who?
GOLEM: Of Joseph.
RIVKA: Oh. She's right. But it's all right. I'm getting more used to it. *(Pause)* How come you're speaking to me, then?
GOLEM: I've made you a present.
RIVKA: Did she order you not to speak to me?
GOLEM: Look.

(The GOLEM holds out a figurine. RIVKA looks at it.)

RIVKA: It's me.
GOLEM: True.
RIVKA: It's very good.
GOLEM: Thank you.
RIVKA: How did you get so good?
GOLEM: I understand clay.
RIVKA: Yes. Of course you do.
GOLEM: I've made two for your mother. One of her, one of Bezalel.
RIVKA: Bezalel? How do you know about Bezalel?
GOLEM: She told me. Maybe he will come back to life, in this.
RIVKA: Don't give her that.
GOLEM: Why not?
RIVKA: It will surprise her. It will make her—unhappy.
GOLEM: Are you sure?
RIVKA: Yes. I'm sure. If necessary, I will order you not to give it to her. *(Pause)* Assuming that means anything. Did Devorah really order you not to talk to me?
GOLEM: They're golems, not idols. Why should they upset her?
RIVKA: You're not answering me. Did she order you not to talk to me?
GOLEM: Do you mind that I'm talking to you?

RIVKA: It's not that, but—
GOLEM: I remember things.
RIVKA: What things? What are you talking about?
GOLEM: Aren't you going to tell me a story, today?
RIVKA: I don't know if that's such a great idea.
GOLEM: Then maybe I'll tell you a story.
RIVKA: You'll tell me a story?
GOLEM: Yes. Why not?
RIVKA: The only stories you know, we've told you.
GOLEM: I can remember others.
RIVKA: What others?
GOLEM: I can remember you.
RIVKA: Golem, tell me, did my sister order you not to speak to me or didn't she?
GOLEM: Call me Joseph.
RIVKA: You are not Joseph.
GOLEM: Rivka.
RIVKA: Answer my question.
GOLEM: You are Rivka.
RIVKA: I'll need to get my father.
GOLEM: Yes, she ordered me.
RIVKA: Then why are you disobeying her?
GOLEM: Do you mind?
RIVKA: I mind that you are disobeying her.
GOLEM: Rivka.
RIVKA: I'll get my father.
GOLEM: I baked a special challah for you, every Friday.
RIVKA: What?
GOLEM: Once, I bought some earrings and hid them inside the challah. You almost broke your tooth, you said.
RIVKA: How do you know this, Golem?
GOLEM: My name is Joseph.
RIVKA: Joseph is dead.
GOLEM: Then why is he standing right in front of you?
(Pause)

RIVKA: You really are a demon.
GOLEM: Yes. And I am Joseph.
RIVKA: How can you be both?
GOLEM: I am possessed.
RIVKA: By what?
GOLEM: Myself.
RIVKA: No. Just one stupid fact about those earrings doesn't prove anything.
GOLEM: You promised to be faithful to me, near the well.
RIVKA: That was the story, not us.
GOLEM: That was us, as well.
RIVKA: You guessed.
GOLEM: He wanted right away to take her.
RIVKA: Joseph would never have spoken to me, like that.
GOLEM: It was from the story.
RIVKA: I have to go.
GOLEM: Your mother has a suitor in mind. You will meet with him, in a few days.
RIVKA: I know.
GOLEM: It's Moshe.
RIVKA: He is a very kind man. My father says he is going to be a rabbi, just like Isaac.
GOLEM: He is not right for you.
RIVKA: How do you know?
GOLEM: Don't tell anyone I spoke to you.
RIVKA: Why not?
GOLEM: I don't think your father would be happy.
RIVKA: You're full of surprises.
GOLEM: It seems that every time I surprise someone, they become unhappy.
RIVKA: You're right.
GOLEM: Rivka.
RIVKA: Yes?
GOLEM: Remember what she did, in the story, when other suitors came?

Scene Eight

MOSHE sits, staring nervously at the GOLEM. The GOLEM stares silently back. They stay like that. The REBBETSIN enters.

REBBETSIN: I'm sorry to keep you waiting, Moshe.
MOSHE: That's all right.
REBBETSIN: Rivka's almost ready.
MOSHE: You don't have to rush.
(The REBBETSIN sits.)
REBBETSIN: So, my husband tells me you are one of his most valued colleagues.
MOSHE: *(Still staring at the GOLEM)* I wouldn't say exactly colleague. Not of the Maharal. I'm more of a student. As are we all.
REBBETSIN: I hope Joseph doesn't make you too nervous.
MOSHE: You actually call it Joseph?
REBBETSIN: I do. Though you'd probably better not call him that in front of Rivka.
MOSHE: Yes...of course not. It's amazing—I just keep thinking of that night. And I can't believe...it could be Joseph sitting there.
REBBETSIN: Did you know Joseph well?
MOSHE: Not well. Mostly from the Yeshiva. I know the Maharal thought a lot of him. I guess that's why Joseph—why Rivka and Joseph were betrothed.
REBBETSIN: The Rabbi thinks a lot of you, as well.
MOSHE: And I think of lot of him. Of course. He's...the Maharal.
(Pause. MOSHE stares at the GOLEM.)
REBBETSIN: Maybe I'd better check on Rivka. Joseph, why don't you wait in the kitchen.
(The GOLEM remains seated.)
Joseph?
(RIVKA enters. Her clothes and hair are a mess. MOSHE stands.)
Rivka, what happened to you?

RIVKA: What do you mean, Mamma?

REBBETSIN: You look—you look—

RIVKA: You don't like it?

REBBETSIN: What happened?

RIVKA: Don't I look pretty, Moshe?

MOSHE: Um, yes, of course.

RIVKA: You see?

REBBETSIN: Maybe you should come back another time, Moshe.

RIVKA: No that's all right. You'll stay, won't you, Moshe?

MOSHE: If you want me to.

RIVKA: I'd love you to.

REBBETSIN: There's no need—

RIVKA: Won't you give us a chance to speak to each other, Mamma?

REBBETSIN: Let me just get you a comb, or something...

RIVKA: I couldn't let Moshe wait any longer, with only Joseph to keep him company. Not very good company, is he, Moshe?

MOSHE: I thought you didn't like to, um—

REBBETSIN: Joseph, I thought I told you to wait in the kitchen.

(The GOLEM exits.)

I'm sorry about this, Moshe.

RIVKA: Please sit down, Moshe. I'll have Joseph bring you some water.

(MOSHE sits.)

MOSHE: I don't really need any—

RIVKA: Mamma, could you leave us alone to talk? We should talk, shouldn't we, Moshe?

MOSHE: Yes, of course.

REBBETSIN: I'm not going to leave you when you're like this.

RIVKA: I'm all right Momma. Really. I'm so sorry. I'm just a little nervous that's all. You can understand that, can't you Moshe?

MOSHE: There's no need…

RIVKA: That's so nice of you to say.

REBBETSIN: She not usually—

RIVKA: You're embarrassing me, Momma. Just because I'm a little nervous. But Moshe understands.

MOSHE: Oh, yes.

RIVKA: See, Momma, no need to worry. You are going to let us alone to talk though, won't you? It would be so rude to Moshe to send him home.

REBBETSIN: Well...all right. But I'm coming back to check on things.

RIVKA: Thank you, Mamma.

(REBBETSIN exits.)

You mustn't mind my mother.

MOSHE: No. I don't.

RIVKA: It's all right. I saw that look you gave her.

MOSHE: What look?

RIVKA: Don't worry, I won't tell her. *(Pause)* Well, don't you speak? You're being as quiet as a golem.

(RIVKA laughs.)

MOSHE: I know, it must be very difficult for you, since Joseph died—

RIVKA: Did he? I could have sworn I just saw him.

MOSHE: I—of course, I mean your betrothed. Your former betrothed.

RIVKA: *(Calling out)* Joseph! You'll see in a minute, he's just fine.

MOSHE: I don't mean—

RIVKA: Joseph!

(The GOLEM enters.)

There he is. You see?

MOSHE: But surely, he's—

RIVKA: All that worry for nothing.

MOSHE: Yes. For nothing.

RIVKA: Joseph, Moshe was worried that you were dead. Can you believe that?

(The GOLEM shakes his head.)

You see, he can't believe it, either.

MOSHE: Do you...talk to him?
RIVKA: Yes, of course. He talks back, too.
MOSHE: He talks?
RIVKA: Listen. Can't you hear him?
(Silence)
MOSHE: I don't hear anything.
RIVKA: He's singing.
MOSHE: He's what?
RIVKA: Tra la la la la—dance, Joseph.
(The GOLEM dances awkwardly.)
Isn't he a wonderful dancer, my Joseph?
MOSHE: Maybe I ought to come again, some other time.
RIVKA: Leaving so soon? But we were supposed to talk.
MOSHE: Perhaps, at another time...
RIVKA: I'll have to stay here and talk to Joseph.
MOSHE: Rivka, I—I know how much you loved Joseph. And maybe you have decided, it would be impossible to care for somebody else. So I won't stay. But I think I could care for you. So if you change your mind about me, I would love to see you again.
(MOSHE gets up to leave.)
RIVKA: Moshe. Thank you. I'm sorry.
MOSHE: It's all right. I understand.
(MOSHE exits.)
RIVKA: That was terrible, what I just did to him.
GOLEM: Was it?
RIVKA: Stop dancing, for goodness sake.
(The GOLEM stops dancing.)
Sometimes I think—I hope to God you are who you say you are.
GOLEM: I accept every blemish found in you.
(The REBBETSIN enters.)
REBBETSIN: Where is he?
RIVKA: Gone.
REBBETSIN: Gone? Gone where? What did you do?

RIVKA: He just wasn't interested, Momma.

REBBETSIN: Oh, I should have never let you… He couldn't have gone far. Let me see if I can talk with him. And when I back, I'm going to have a talk with you, Rivka.

(REBBETSIN exits.)

GOLEM: Is she upset?

RIVKA: Yes. *(She laughs.)* Yes, she's upset.

GOLEM: Why does that make you laugh?

RIVKA: I don't know.

GOLEM: Rivka.

RIVKA: Yes?

GOLEM: Call me Joseph.

RIVKA: I don't know…

GOLEM: You just did. To Moshe.

RIVKA: Yes. It's true. I know.

GOLEM: I love you, Rivka.

RIVKA: Oh.

GOLEM: Here.

(He gives her a clay figure.)

RIVKA: What is it?

GOLEM: A little golem. To remember me by.

RIVKA: Why? What's going to happen to you?

GOLEM: Demons never seem to live till the end of the story.

(The REBBETSIN enters.)

RIVKA: I'm sorry, Momma.

REBBETSIN: Shhh.

RIVKA: What? What is it?

REBBETSIN: They just said…I just heard…

RIVKA: What is it, Mamma?

REBBETSIN: Golem, we need your help.

GOLEM: What do you want me to do?

REBBETSIN: They've arrested Devorah. They're calling her a witch. And they're saying that she killed two babies. You know what that means.

RIVKA: Oh my God.

GOLEM: They're going to kill her.

REBBETSIN: You have to stop them, Golem. You have to save her.

GOLEM: How?

REBBETSIN: Do what ever you have to, I don't care. She will be tied to a well, in the middle of the city. It won't be hard to find. There will be a mob around it, I'm sure. There's always... *(She stops, unable to continue.)* Please, Golem, you must save her. That is your job. You are our protector.

RIVKA: No! You can't just send him out into danger like that.

REBBETSIN: What are you talking about? She's your sister, Rivka.

RIVKA: Let me go. Let me try to stop them.

REBBETSIN: What do you think you're going to do against a mob, Rivka? The Golem is our only hope. Don't worry. This is why your father built him. So he could help protect us. So that he could save Devorah.

RIVKA: But what if he can't?

REBBETSIN: He can. I know he can. Can't you, Joseph?

GOLEM: I'll do my best.

REBBETSIN: Then go. Go quickly.

GOLEM: Don't I get to kiss my love goodbye?

REBBETSIN: This is not a story, Golem. This is real. This is the time for you to do your duty.

GOLEM: But I love her.

REBBETSIN: Enough of this madness. Go.

GOLEM: I'm sorry. Yes, maybe I'm mad. Or maybe I'm just feigning madness.

RIVKA: Joseph.

GOLEM: Yes?

RIVKA: Come back safely, Joseph.

(The GOLEM exits.)

Scene Nine

RUDOLF and the MAHARAL are talking.

MAHARAL: It is no coincidence that Devorah is my daughter. Thaddeus hates me, and he's trying to attack me. First through Joseph, now through Devorah. He doesn't dare attack me directly, because he knows we're friendly, and he's afraid of you. But now he's calling Devorah a witch. You know what that means.

RUDOLF: Is she one?

MAHARAL: No. Of course not.

RUDOLF: But she reads. When they found her in the synagogue, she was writing out mystical figures.

MAHARAL: Most people read, in our community. Men and women, both. Devorah wasn't writing down any sort of mystical figures. She helps with the accounting. Just because she was writing in Hebrew, they thought it was mystical.

RUDOLF: And then they found those babies. Two of them this time, in the synagogue.

MAHARAL: Which is she? A murderer or a witch?

RUDOLF: Both, they say.

MAHARAL: She is neither.

RUDOLF: I've met a few witches. Fascinating women. But it's against Christian law, of course, and the Jesuits won't allow that. Thaddeus particularly.

MAHARAL: It's against Jewish law, too. Devorah is no witch.

RUDOLF: What about the Kabala?

MAHARAL: That's different.

RUDOLF: It doesn't seem that different.

MAHARAL: Devorah knows nothing of the Kabala. And she is certainly no murderer.

RUDOLF: Then who did kill those babies?

MAHARAL: I don't know. But my daughter is innocent, I assure you.

(Pause)

RUDOLF: They say there is a demon that lives in your house. Some say a demon, others a ghost, and still others say both.

MAHARAL: Perhaps. Of sorts.

RUDOLF: It's true then?

MAHARAL: He has a human spirit. And his only function is to protect us. We need protection.

RUDOLF: Is he in the room?

MAHARAL: Do you see him?

RUDOLF: For all I know, he could be invisible.

MAHARAL: No, he isn't here. He is just a man made of clay, that's all.

RUDOLF: That's all? It seems like a lot, to me. Is this what you call a gollum?

MAHARAL: A golem, yes. I'm surprised you know the word.

RUDOLF: I've read a lot about demons. If you summon him, will he injure me?

MAHARAL: No, of course not.

RUDOLF: Then please do so. I would be very curious to see a golem in person.

MAHARAL: If you like. Joseph!

RUDOLF: Joseph! Then the spirit of that boy is in him?

MAHRAL: Yes.

RUDOLF: That sounds terribly dangerous to me. Where is he? Doesn't he come when you call?

MAHARAL: He usually does. Joseph!

RUDOLF: Why did you create such a thing?

MAHARAL: I was given a prophetic dream, and it advised me that the Jewish people needed a defender.

RUDOLF: When was this?

MAHARAL: Right after we met, last time.

RUDOLF: And I agreed to help you.

MAHARAL: And my disciple, Joseph, was killed.

RUDOLF: I did my best to bring his killers to justice. These things take time.

MAHARAL: I know. That is why we need a defender. Joseph was stoned to death, and now my daughter has been arrested for witchery. And if you don't do anything about it, she will be killed too.

RUDOLF: She will be tried.

MAHARAL: You may have changed the trials for the men of the Jewish community, but a witch trial is a witch trial. The trial itself will kill her, you know that. Please, your majesty, you must save her. You're the only one who can do it.

RUDOLF: What about your demon?

MAHARAL: I prefer to appeal to you.

RUDOLF: Why? Is the demon not powerful enough?

MAHARAL: I don't know. I'm not sure what the extent of his powers are. But I'm not willing to take any chances. This is my daughter we're talking about.

RUDOLF: I don't know, Judah. It's hard to defend you when they say you consort with demons, and it turns out to be true. Not that I'm judgmental. Do what you wish. But the law is the law, and it looks bad. It looks bad for me.

MAHARAL: Please. Consider my request. You've met Devorah. Please, do not let her die. She is innocent, I assure you.

RUDOLF: On one condition.

MAHARAL: Which is?

RUDOLF: You must get rid of your demon. I cannot continue to help you if you keep him.

MAHARAL: But my dream—

RUDOLF: I cannot afford that kind of embarrassment, in court. I have become known as an advocate for the Jews, ever since I lifted the trade barriers against your people.

MAHARAL: I know. I appreciated that.

RUDOLF: I'll tell you the truth. Since these rumors of demons have surfaced, people are calling for the expulsion of your people, for good this time. Unless you get rid of your demon, I won't be able to oppose them. My position in court is fragile these days, and it doesn't help that I constantly give aid to Jews and witches. But not demons. There's a limit, Judah.

MAHARAL: And if I don't?

RUDOLF: This is not a request, Judah, it's an order from your King. If he continues to live, I cannot interfere on Devorah's behalf. And I will not continue to protect the Jews.

MAHARAL: Very well. Of course, I will do as you request.

RUDOLF: Good.

MAHARAL: Please, I just ask that you act quickly. My daughter's life is at stake.

RUDOLF: I won't let anything happen to her, as long as you keep your side of the bargain. In the meantime, I suggest you work on discovering who has killed these last two babies. And find this demon of yours soon.

MAHARAL: I will. Thank you.

(RUDOLF grabs his dark cloak, covers up his royal vestments and hides his face in the hood, then exits.)

MAHARAL: Joseph! Where are you?

(RIVKA enters.)

RIVKA: Are you going to kill him?

MAHARAL: Rivka, do you know where Joseph is?

RIVKA: Pappa, are you going to kill him?

MAHARAL: Where is he?

RIVKA: Trying to save my sister's life.

MAHARAL: Saving Devorah? We must stop him at once. I need to find the incantation to call him back.

(He goes to his books and starts searching.)

RIVKA: I heard your conversation with King Rudolf.

MAHARAL: You shouldn't eavesdrop.

RIVKA: You agreed to kill Joseph.

MAHARAL: No, I didn't.

RIVKA: You didn't?

MAHARAL: No. He was never really alive. Ah, here it is.

(The MAHARAL pick up a book. The REBBETSIN enters.)

REBBETSIN: Has there been any word, yet?

RIVKA: Pappa wants to kill Joseph.

REBBETSIN: Judah, is this true?

MAHARAL: It's the only way to save Devorah. The King agreed to save her, but he insists that I destroy the Golem. And maybe he's right. Maybe it was a bad idea to bring a demon into this world, even for our protection.

RIVKA: He's going to save Devorah? Like he saved Joseph?

MAHARAL: Please, Rivka, I have to concentrate.

REBBETSIN: But Judah, Rivka's right. How do we know she won't be killed, like Joseph was? The King promised to save him, too.

RIVKA: Will he do anything to stop her from getting stoned, the way they stoned Joseph?

MAHARAL: He cannot control everything.

RIVKA: He cannot control anything. The day after you saw the King last time, Joseph was killed.

MAHARAL: Please, he's doing the best that he can.

REBBETSIN: Maybe we should trust the Golem, not the King. Not this time.

MAHARAL: Pearla, he can bleed. You saw it yourself. And that stone—he told you it was just a trick. What if he can't save her? He's so unpredictable...Who knows what he will do. Something happened when I created him, something wrong I think. At least we know King Rudolf can free her from her trial. After that...we will have to try to protect her ourselves. We'll hide her, if we must. Or we'll send her to Poland, to be with Isaac.

REBBETSIN: Are you sure, Judah?

MAHARAL: It's our only choice, I think. *(The MAHARAL picks up his book and starts reading.)* I call you to me, Joseph Golem, I, your creator, who wrote the word *Emet* on your forehead and allowed God to give you life. Hear my voice and come to me as I chant the 88-syllable name of God found within the Sephira Gevurah.

(The MAHARAL begins to chant, and the sound of wind is heard.)

RIVKA: Please, stop, Pappa. Please, Pappa, let him live.

(The MAHARAL continues to chant.)

MAHARAL: He is here.

(The GOLEM enters. He carries a bloody, wrapped bundle.)

RIVKA: Joseph, go!

MAHARAL: What are you carrying?

GOLEM: I have killed someone.

REBBETSIN: Is Devorah all right?

GOLEM: Devorah is free. I freed her. She's all right.

REBBETSIN: Thank you. Thank you, Golem.

RIVKA: I knew it, Pappa. I knew he would save her.

MAHARAL: Whom did you kill?

GOLEM: Will you bury the body? I fear they will destroy me.

REBBETSIN: What happened?

GOLEM: I found the man who has been killing all the children. It was Thaddeus. I thought I was just touching him, just brushing him. But then my demon strength grew in me, and I knew what I had to do.

REBBETSIN: You killed Thaddeus.

GOLEM: He was evil. So very evil. We would never have been safe, while he was alive.

MAHARAL: He was deluded, and he did evil things, it's true. But that's no excuse for killing him.

GOLEM: I am made for violence. I was carved out of the earth, to protect the Jewish people in any way necessary. It was inevitable that things would end this way.

MAHARAL: Perhaps that's true. Perhaps it's my fault.

RIVKA: So what Thaddeus is dead. Better him than Devorah.

GOLEM: Will you bury the body? I fear they are going to arrest me. They think I am a murderer.

MAHARAL: You are a murderer.

RIVKA: He saved Devorah. Doesn't that count for anything?

MAHARAL: Perhaps he saved her. For the moment. And I'm grateful for that. But he's put us in terrible danger, more danger than ever. Alive, Thaddeus would have been our best witness, our best argument for the untruth of their accusations. Dead, he will just bring more persecutions. He was a respected man. The reprisals will go on and on.

GOLEM: Will you bury the body?

MAHARAL: King Rudolf will be furious. It will be harder than ever to convince him to protect us. And Devorah...we will have to send her to Poland.

REBBETSIN: But if the King sees that you've done what he asked...

RIVKA: No!

MAHARAL: Lie down, Joseph.

RIVKA: No, Joseph, don't do it.

MAHARAL: Joseph, I command you, lie down.

RIVKA: Please, don't kill him, Pappa. Please. He didn't mean to kill Thaddeus. He didn't know it was wrong.

MAHARAL: Lie down!

GOLEM: No.

MAHARAL: What?

(The GOLEM puts the bloody body down and stares at them. They back up a little.)

GOLEM: No.

MAHARAL: You must obey my command. Lie down.

REBBETSIN: Lie down, Golem. Do as Judah tells you.

GOLEM: I won't.

MAHARAL: By the four elements, by the 99-syllable name of God, found within the Sephira Malkut, I command it.

(The MAHARAL begins chanting, and the GOLEM is pushed slowly towards the floor.)

RIVKA: No!

(She runs over and holds the GOLEM up.)

REBETTSIN: Let go of him, Rivka. It's not right to grab a man like that.

GOLEM: You know, every time this happens to me, I am amazed at the suddenness. Last time it was even faster. The cries of anger, the sound of stones breaking glass, and then nothing.

RIVKA: This is murder.

REBBETSIN: Don't say that, dear, don't say that. Your father wouldn't do anything like that. Maybe the Golem reminds us of the people we once loved, like Bezalel and Joseph, but we must not forget he's a demon inside. Perhaps I let myself forget that once or twice, but it's true.

RIVKA: Don't give up, Joseph. Pappa, stop it. You're killing Joseph. Please, don't make him die again. I love him.

GOLEM: You do?

RIVKA: Yes.

GOLEM: All right, Rivka.

RIVKA: All right?

(The GOLEM kisses her. The MAHARAL stops chanting.)

MAHARAL: Pull them apart! Pull them apart! He may be taking her soul.

(The REBBETSIN and the MAHARAL grab the GOLEM and pull him away from RIVKA surprisingly easily. The GOLEM and RIVKA stare at each other.)

GOLEM: I'm alive, Judah.

(The MAHARAL wipes away the aleph on the GOLEM's forehead. With a very real scream, the GOLEM collapses. RIVKA realizes what the MAHARAL is doing, too late.)

RIVKA: No!

MAHARAL: It is done.

RIVKA: How did you…

MAHARAL: I have removed the letter aleph, and now *Met* is written on his forehead. It means death, as you know.

RIVKA: You mean you—just one letter, and it killed him? Bring him back. Write the letter back on his forehead, if that's all the difference there is between life and death.

MAHARAL: No. Maybe some other rabbi will raise a new golem one day, if one is needed again. Or maybe he will not. Maybe it would be wiser not to bring another golem into this world.

RIVKA: Than I'll write it. Give me your books, and I'll raise him myself.

MAHARAL: It's not as simple as that. Once the word death is on his forehead, it can never be changed, any more than it can be changed for you or me.

RIVKA: No! Joseph!

(DEVORAH enters.)

REBBETSIN: Devorah! You're all right, like the Golem said. Thank God you weren't recaptured.

MAHARAL: We'll have to hide you immediately.

DEVORAH: Hide me? What's going on? What happened to the Golem?

RIVKA: Pappa murdered him.

REBBETSIN: Hush, dear. The Rabbi turned the Golem back into clay. He had no choice. The Golem killed Thaddeus.

DEVORAH: Thaddeus? I don't think that's possible.

MAHARAL: Why not?

DEVORAH: The Golem didn't kill anybody.

MAHARAL: Then what's in the bag?

DEVORAH: Two piglets. Thaddeus had planted them in the synagogue, claiming that they were two babies I had killed with my witchcraft. But when the Golem found the bag and showed everyone that there were piglets inside, they let me free. Thaddeus still claimed I was a witch, but no one believed him after that.

(The MAHARAL checks the bag.)

REBBETSIN: So the whole story about the dead babies was a lie?

DEVORAH: Yes. Didn't the Golem tell you any of this?

MAHARAL: It's true. They're just pigs, inside.

REBBETSIN: So then...you're safe? I mean, nobody's after you?

DEVORAH: I'm safe. And I don't think people will be so quick to believe Thaddeus in the future.

REBBETSIN: Then the Golem really did save you.

DEVORAH: Yes, he did.

REBBETSIN: Then why did he tell us that story about killing someone?

RIVKA: He was testing us. Like in that story, about the true friend.

REBBETSIN: Oh yes, that one.

RIVKA: So you killed him for nothing.

MAHARAL: He was dangerous, nonetheless. And the King would never have forgiven me, if I hadn't turned him back into clay. It was necessary.

REBBETSIN: He tried to take away your soul.

RIVKA: He kissed me. And he wasn't even strong enough to fight off the two of you.

MAHARAL: My dear, he was just clay. Clay cannot die, because clay cannot live.

RIVKA: But why are you saying this? You've seen him walk, and talk, and think, and feel. What else is life?

MAHARAL: He was a tool, sent to us by God, to save us. And he did save us. He truly did. And now his mission is complete. That's all he was here for.

RIVKA: He lived. You called him Joseph. He had a name.

MAHARAL: It looked like Joseph, it is true. And maybe, somehow, Joseph helped us in one final way. You should be grateful for that.

RIVKA: It's not just a story, Pappa. He was real. He was real.

REBBETSIN: He was real once.

DEVORAH: I will always be thankful for the way he saved me. He was a great warrior.

MAHARAL: A soldier for the Jewish cause.

RIVKA: Doesn't anyone remember him as he really was?

REBBETSIN: Of course we do. We all do. Try not to be too sad, my dear. Think of what wonderful stories we will be able to tell about him, someday.

RIVKA: Joseph? Joseph? Joseph?

(Blackout)

The Living Methuselah

Original Production

The Living Methuselah was presented by Untitled Theater Company #61 at Theater 22 in New York City in February 1997. It was directed and designed by Edward Einhorn; David A. Einhorn was the producer; J. P. Klein was the assistant director; David Maxine served as the scenic design consultant. The cast was as follows:

METHUSELAH .... Jason Harris
SERACH .... Erin Kelley
HANDMAIDEN 1 .... Mira Kingsley
DOCTOR .... Daniel Leventritt
HANDMAIDEN 2 .... Julia Martin

The Living Methuselah

METHUSELAH is lying on his bed (a hospital bed might be appropriate). His wife, SERACH, is anxiously attending to him.

METHUSELAH: Bastard.
SERACH: Not this again.
METHUSELAH: Who does he think he is?
SERACH: It's just a song.
METHUSELAH: "But who calls that livin'—"
SERACH: Methuselah—
METHUSELAH: "When no gal will give in—"
SERACH: Thusy—
METHUSELAH: "To no man what's nine hundred years."
SERACH: He didn't know what he was talking about.
METHUSELAH: Age makes a man more handsome, not less.
SERACH: I gave in, didn't I, Thusy?
METHUSELAH: I was younger then.
SERACH: You were nine hundred. At least nine hundred.
METHUSELAH: He didn't even give me my right age. Nine hundred years. Plenty of people have lived nine hundred years. Even that idiot grandson of mine lived nine hundred years. And my grandfather. He almost outlived me, he did. He lived nine hundred and sixty-two years. Clever old coot. And I'll tell you, he was no slouch with women either. Neither was I. Especially when I was nine hundred.
SERACH: I fell for you immediately. It was love at first sight. My beautiful Methuselah. Thusy.

METHUSELAH: Would you stop calling me that insipid nickname?
SERACH: It's not insipid, it's a nice nickname.
METHUSELAH: Why don't you call me Meth? Or Uselah?
SERACH: It's a term of endearment.
METHUSELAH: Or Ethus? Or just Jack, for God's sake?
SERACH: I wish you had a nickname for me.
METHUSELAH: I do. I call you old bitch.
SERACH: That's not a term of endearment. That's horrible.
METHUSELAH: *(chuckling)* Old bitch.
SERACH: Stop it.
METHUSELAH: Come here, old bitch, I want to bang you one. *(He tries to grab her. She avoids him.)*
SERACH: Methuselah!
(He subsides. Pause. METHUSELAH closes his eyes. SERACH shakes him, worried.)
Methuselah?
METHUSELAH: Can't I have any rest?
SERACH: Sorry, I was just worried—
METHUSELAH: Thought I'd bought the farm, eh?
SERACH: I just thought you were—
METHUSELAH: Thought I'd kicked the can? Thought it was time for me to start pushin' up the daisies, is that it?
SERACH: It's just that the doctor said—
METHUSELAH: I've faced greater odds.
SERACH: I know.
METHUSELAH: Did I ever tell you about the flood?
SERACH: I remember.
METHUSELAH: My own grandson, mind you. "Two of every kind." "What, do you already have two nine-hundred and sixty-nine year old men on that ark of yours?" I asked. He didn't have much of an answer for that. Goddamn nerve.
SERACH: You shouldn't excite yourself so.
METHUSELAH: Why not?
SERACH: The doctor—

METHUSELAH: The hell with the doctor.

(The DOCTOR enters. He is carrying a chart, which he examines unhappily.)

DOCTOR: I'm afraid I have some bad news for you, sir.

METHUSELAH: What, another organ gone bad?

DOCTOR: In a way, but that's not—

METHUSELAH: Cancer?

DOCTOR: Well, yes, but that's not the whole of it, sir.

METHUSELAH: A heart attack? A stroke? AIDS?

DOCTOR: Yes, those too, but I'm afraid—

METHUSELAH: Lou Gehrig's disease? The Ebola virus? Small Pox?

DOCTOR: Please, sir—

METHUSELAH: The Black Plague? The Red Death? The Martian Flu?

DOCTOR: All these things are true, yes, I've diagnosed them all, but I'm afraid this time it's more serious.

METHUSELAH: Get away from me. I don't want to hear it.

DOCTOR: But, sir—

METHUSELAH: You're a doctor, so cure it. Now go away.

SERACH: It's okay, doctor, tell me, I want to know.

METHUSELAH: Stop flirting with him.

SERACH: I'm not flirting, I'm worried about you.

METHUSELAH: I know all about you two.

SERACH: There's nothing to know.

METHUSELAH: I see the way he looks at you. He's just waiting for me to die. Well, he'll have to wait a little longer.

DOCTOR: Methuselah, how old are you?

METHUSELAH: Nine-hundred and sixty-nine years old.

DOCTOR: You've lived a full life.

METHUSELAH: It's not a full life till I reach a thousand. At least.

SERACH: He's really much older.

METHUSELAH: I am not.

SERACH: It's ridiculous. He's afraid to admit he's over a thousand. He's afraid of getting old.

METHUSELAH: Liar.

SERACH: He's been saying he's nine hundred and sixty-nine for as long as I've know him, which is over two thousand years.

METHUSELAH: Which makes *you* how old?

SERACH: A lady doesn't tell her age.

METHUSELAH: *(Chuckling)* You see. As long as I'm nine hundred and sixty-nine, you can pretend you're even younger than that. It's in your interest, too.

DOCTOR: I'm afraid your body has simply run its course, sir. The human body is just a machine. It had to run down, eventually.

METHUSELAH: Then get me a new body.

DOCTOR: I can't do that, sir.

METHUSELAH: Why not? It's just a machine, like you said. They got me a new liver, a new heart, a new appendix—that was money down the drain, how was I to know the damn things would just keep bursting—new intestines, a new spleen, a new brain, one doctor even gave me a new outlook on life, or so he said. Compared to that, a new body should be childsplay.

DOCTOR: It's not just that.

METHUSELAH: Well? What else is it?

DOCTOR: It's—you. You can't go on forever, you know. Every being has an ending point, a terminus, a final breath. Even the universe has an end. Do you think you will live longer than the universe?

METHUSELAH: Why not? The universe is a mess. I keep myself fit, at least.

SERACH: You should exercise more.

METHUSELAH: Why are you such a nag?

SERACH: And eat better.

METHUSELAH: Nag, nag, nag, that's all she's done, since I married her.

DOCTOR: I'm afraid the clock has begun ticking, for you.

METHUSELAH: Well then, turn it off. Don't wind the damn thing, or take out its batteries.

DOCTOR: You have one day left to live.

(The DOCTOR exits.)

METHUSELAH: You see? That's why I won't go to doctors. All they ever want to do is kill you.

(SERACH starts crying.)

Oh, for God's sake. Old bitch?

(SERACH keeps crying.)

Serach?

SERACH: Yes, my darling?

METHUSELAH: I'll tell you a story. You like my stories. Do you want me to tell you one?

SERACH: Please.

METHUSELAH: Well then, dry your eyes, for goodness sakes.

SERACH: I'm sorry.

METHUSELAH: I wish I still had my handmaidens. They were so much more sensible. Not so sentimental.

(The HANDMAIDENS enter. They are beautiful.)

And so beautiful.

SERACH: Thusy?

METHUSELAH: Shall I tell you about my bastard grandson, then?

SERACH: Yes, do.

METHUSELAH: Ungrateful son-of-a-bitch. He said I was wicked. Just because God had spoken to him, and not to me. I didn't tell him God had tried to speak to me, but I hadn't listened. In those days, God would talk to anyone who was half willing to pay attention.

(Suddenly, METHUSELAH is back in the time of the Flood. A bright light shines on him.)

HANDMAIDENS: Methuselah!

METHUSELAH: What is it?

HANDMAIDENS: Methuselah, wake up!

METHUSELAH: Are you crazy? It's the middle of the night.

HANDMAIDENS: It's God, Methuselah.

METHUSELAH: Yes, I had guessed that one.

HANDMAIDENS: I have determined to make an end to all flesh, for the earth is filled with violence through them; behold, I will destroy them with the earth.

METHUSELAH: The end of all flesh? Are you serious? What sort of solution is that? You don't like us, so you're just going to kill us all off?

HANDMAIDENS: Make yourself an ark of gopher wood; make rooms in the ark, and cover it inside and out with pitch.

METHUSELAH: I'm really not much of a carpenter.

HANDMAIDENS: This is how you are to make it: the length of the ark three hundred cubits—

METHUSELAH: Wait a second, wait a second, let me write this down. *(Grabbing a pen and pad)* So its length is how many cubits?

HANDMAIDENS: Three hundred.

METHUSELAH: Are you sure about this?

HANDMAIDENS: Yes, it's three hundred.

METHUSELAH: No, I mean this end of all flesh thing?

HANDMAIDENS: I am sure.

METHUSELAH: What about the animals?

HANDMAIDENS: Two of each will be saved.

METHUSELAH: Just two?

HANDMAIDENS: Do not question me.

(Thunder is heard.)

METHUSELAH: I'm sorry, God, I just can't go along with this. I mean, I know this makes me wicked, or whatever, but I can't possibly believe that everyone else in the world deserves to die. I mean, I have grandchildren. And great-grandchildren. And a wife. And some handmaidens. They might not be perfect, certainly Noah is a self-righteous pain in the ass, but even he doesn't deserve to die. Plus, I'd never get that ark thing done. You know how I am. I'd start it, get distracted, start another project, and before you know it a hundred years will have gone by. *(Silence)* God? *(Silence)* God?

(METHUSELAH rolls over and goes to sleep. HANDMAIDEN 1 walks up to him and shakes him.)

HANDMAIDEN 1: It's raining, Methuselah.

METHUSELAH: Is it really you? Are you really alive?

HANDMAIDEN 1: Yes, Methuselah. I am now. But soon I'm going to drown.

METHUSELAH: Drown? But that's not how you died. I remember...you died from...how did you die?

HANDMAIDEN 1: It's raining. You have to get up and pack. It's going to flood.

METHUSELAH: Flood? Oh, the Flood! It's the Flood!

(He allows himself to be pulled out of bed. The DOCTOR enters.)

DOCTOR: What he is experiencing is severe delusions, in which the actions of the past seem to be taking place in his present. This is also known as having your life flash before your eyes. For the normal man, this may merely take a few minutes, but, in light of his extreme age, I would expect it to take considerably longer.

SERACH: Is there nothing you can do for him?

DOCTOR: Watch. Participate.

METHUSELAH: Noah, you bastard. What do you think you're doing?

DOCTOR: Getting ready to set sail.

METHUSELAH: Why didn't you tell me it was time?

DOCTOR: You will not be needed, on this ark.

METHUSELAH: Of course you need me, I'm your grandfather.

DOCTOR: You are wicked.

METHUSELAH: Not in comparison to the rest of the people of the world. They're really terrible. I could tell you some stories—

DOCTOR: I can only take two of every kind of animal with me.

METHUSELAH: And I said to him—

SERACH: What, do you already have two nine hundred and sixty-nine year old men on that ark of yours?

METHUSELAH: Have I told you this one before?

DOCTOR: I'm sorry. I cannot help you.

(The DOCTOR exits.)

METHUSELAH: Idiot. Well, what do you expect from a man who names his three sons Ham, Shemp and Curly?

SERACH: Their names were Ham, Shem and Japheth.

METHUSELAH: Sure, take his side.

HANDMAIDEN 2: Methuselah, what shall we do? The waters are rising higher and higher. Half the houses are already engulfed. Soon, we shall be covered, too, even up on this hill.

METHUSELAH: Are you alive, too?

HANDMAIDEN 2: Methuselah, please save us!

METHUSELAH: I wanted to, I promise you. But there was nothing I could do.

HANDMAIDEN 2: Save us from the Flood!

METHUSELAH: The Flood? No, you died from…something. Something else.

HANDMAIDEN 2: I haven't died yet. But I will if you don't help me.

METHUSELAH: How can I help you? I don't even have an ark. We'll just have to wait for the waters to reach us.

HANDMAIDEN 2: You must have some ideas. God told you this is coming. Why didn't you prepare?

METHUSELAH: Maybe it will stop raining, soon. It looks like it's going to clear up, to me.

HANDMAIDEN 2: The weatherman predicted rain for the next forty days.

METHUSELAH: Well, what's that big thing, over there?

HANDMAIDEN 2: You mean Mount Ararat?

METHUSELAH: Yes, that. The flood certainly won't reach the top of that. All we have to do is climb up it, and we'll be fine.

HANDMAIDENS: And so Methuselah began climbing Mount Ararat. Every day and every night, for thirty-nine days, he climbed. The waters lapped at his feet as he traveled, but he was always able to keep a step ahead. Finally, he reached the summit; but the waters kept rising, and the rain kept coming. Soon, it rose past his knees, then his waist, then his shoulders. Finally, he was forced to stick his nose in the air, in order to breathe. Then, at the end of the fortieth night, one drop before it would have fully engulfed him, it stopped.

METHUSELAH: It was damned uncomfortable, I'll tell you. When you're over nine hundred years old, the last thing you want to do is stand nose deep in water for a couple of months. And I'm not even getting into the sunburn.

(The DOCTOR enters.)

DOCTOR: I'm afraid you're suffering from hypothermia, starvation and sunstroke. You won't live to see another birthday.

METHUSELAH: Fortunately, it was at that time that I decided to stop having birthdays.

DOCTOR: *(Looking at watch)* Twenty-three hours and fifty minutes.

(The DOCTOR and the HANDMAIDENS exit.)

METHUSELAH: I wish the flood had gotten him. How did he survive the flood, tell me that?

SERACH: He wasn't really there. Nor were the handmaidens. It was just you.

METHUSELAH: Just me, all alone, on top of Mount Ararat, for half a year?

SERACH: Yes.

METHUSELAH: I must have been bored out of my skull. That can't be true. I must have saved someone besides myself.

SERACH: You tried. Those who wanted to follow you could not. They slipped and fell, one by one, into the waters below.

METHUSELAH: How do you know this?

SERACH: You told me once. Long ago.

METHUSELAH: Then I'm the only one. Noah, Ham, Shemp, Curly, they all died long ago. I'm the only one who's lived since before the flood. I'm the only one who saw God destroy the world. Almost. Everyone on the ark survived, for a little while at least. And me.

SERACH: Yes. You're the oldest man there is.

METHUSELAH: I made up a word for it once. Antediluvian. I'm antediluvian. Everybody else is postdiluvian, but I'm antediluvian.

SERACH: You didn't make it up. That was someone else.

METHUSELAH: No. That's impossible. Somebody else made up a word that only applies to me? Who else would make a word like that up? Was it you?

SERACH: No. I don't know who it was.

METHUSELAH: It must have been my handmaidens.

SERACH: You never had handmaidens.

METHUSELAH: I had them once. Maybe they weren't antediluvian. They must have been postdiluvian.

SERACH: No. They were neither.

METHUSELAH: Wait, I remember now. Gomorrah! Oh, that was a time. Talk about a fin de siecle feeling. And Lot was the worst of us.

(The DOCTOR enters, his arms around the HANDMAIDENS.)

DOCTOR: Hey, old man, how are you doing?

METHUSELAH: Who are these two beautiful women?

DOCTOR: To tell the truth, old man, they're my two daughters, but you'd never know it, hey?

METHUSELAH: Your daughters? And the three of you are...

DOCTOR: They tricked me into it. Got me so drunk I didn't know what I was doing, or who I was doing it with, if you know what I mean.

SERACH: Wait, I thought that happened after Sodom and Gomorrah were destroyed.

METHUSELAH: Pedant.

DOCTOR: So, you going to the big party Friday night?
METHUSELAH: Which one? It seems like all we have around here are big parties.
DOCTOR: This one's even bigger. They'll have everyone there. I mean everyone. Sodomites, Gomorrhists. We'll all get to *know* one another, as the biblical saying goes.
METHUSELAH: I don't know. I think God might disapprove. God can be kind of uptight about this kind of thing, I'll tell you from experience. I told you the story of the great Flood—
DOCTOR: Yeah, yeah, yeah, we've all heard. But he promised never to do that again, didn't he? So we're safe.
METHUSELAH: I guess...
DOCTOR: They'll be handmaidens there.
METHUSELAH: Handmaidens?
DOCTOR: By the handful.
METHUSELAH: What time's the party?
(The HANDMAIDENS leave the DOCTOR and line up behind METHUSELAH. There's a lighting change. Music cuts in.)
DOCTOR: And now announcing Methuselah and the Methusalettes.
METHUSELAH: Ain't gonna die,
Just gonna live.
'Cause I've got plenty more
Lovin' to give.
Hope the kiddies
Remember my name,
But I'm gonna be here
Just the same—
'Cause I'm Methuselah.
HANDMAIDENS: He's Methuselah.
METHUSELAH: I'm old Methuselah.
HANDMAIDENS: He's Methuselah.
METHUSELAH: I'm Methuselah, baby, and I'm gonna live some more.
Lived through the plague.

Lived through the flood.
Many a foe has
Wanted my blood.
Stab me to death.
Cut off my head.
Damn it that old man
Should be dead,
But I'm Methuselah.

HANDMAIDENS: He's Methuselah.

METHUSELAH: I'm old Methuselah.

HANDMAIDENS: He's Methuselah.

METHUSELAH: I'm Methuselah, baby, and I'm gonna live some more.
Maybe some day
I'm gonna be sick.
Call in the doctor,
Gets here real quick.
Tells me my life's
Soon at an end—
I say doctor you do not
Comprehend
That I'm Methuselah.

HANDMAIDENS: He's Methuselah.

METHUSELAH: I'm old Methuselah.

HANDMAIDENS: He's Methuselah.

METHUSELAH: I'm Methuselah, baby, and I'm gonna live some more.
(Music ends. METHUSELAH turns to SERACH.)
That's what I call a song. Not that stupid Gershwin stuff.
(HANDMAIDEN 2 runs over to him and hands him a pad, which he autographs.)
What's your name, darling?

HANDMAIDEN 2: Hagar.

METHUSELAH: And what do you do, Hagar?

HANDMAIDEN 2: I'm just a handmaiden.

METHUSELAH: Really?

SERACH: It's amazing. The oldest living human, and you're still having the same fantasies you had at sixteen.

METHUSELAH: Have you seen Lot around here, tonight?

HANDMAIDEN 2: I think he left, already.

METHUSELAH: He left? Where did he go?

HANDMAIDEN 2: Some angel came by, I think.

METHUSELAH: An angel? Why did an angel come by?

HANDMAIDEN 2: I don't know. Something about us all being sinful, and having to destroy our whole city. He said there weren't even ten good men. If there were ten good men, he said, he'd save the city. I said, you've been going to the wrong parties. Come to one of mine, and I'll show you ten good men. He didn't even laugh. You know how those angels can be.

(HANDMAIDEN 1 runs over.)

HANDMAIDEN 1: Can I have your autograph?

METHUSELAH: So he's left the city?

HANDMAIDEN 2: I think so. Why?

METHUSELAH: I've got to go.

HANDMAIDEN 1: But the party's just beginning. It's going to last all night.

METHUSELAH: Come with me. Both of you. I can save you. God's going to destroy the city.

HANDMAIDEN 2: I know, I heard. Kaaa-pow!.

HANDMAIDEN 1: Kaaa-poo-eee!

METHUSELAH: I'm serious.

HANDMAIDEN 1: Then you'd better come with me. I don't want to die a virgin.

HANDMAIDEN 2: Me neither.

METHUSELAH: Listen, you have to believe me. I've seen him do worse. Come with me, before it's too late.

HANDMAIDEN 2: But it's already too late. That angel said the city's going to be destroyed at midnight. It's one minute to midnight now.

METHUSELAH: So we have one minute?

HANDMAIDENS: Uh huh.

(The HANDMAIDENS laugh. METHUSELAH steps away from them.)

METHUSELAH: I renounce this city, its sins, and everything within it!

(The HANDMAIDENS suddenly freeze. METHUSELAH walks over to them and touches them tentatively. They are immobile. He licks his finger. He looks over to SERACH.)

Salt. They were just salt.

SERACH: I know.

METHUSELAH: I hear the town was destroyed behind me, destroyed in fire and brimstone. If I had looked back, I would have become a pillar of salt, myself.

SERACH: But you didn't.

METHUSELAH: Because I couldn't bear to think of all those people, frozen there. How could I have renounced them all? I was one of them. And then I doomed them.

SERACH: You didn't doom them. You saved yourself.

METHUSELAH: I would have doomed them, if I had to, to save myself. I would have turned them into salt myself, to save my own skin.

SERACH: They were wicked.

METHUSELAH: So was I.

SERACH: You didn't do anything. You didn't do anything wrong.

METHUSELAH: I told myself I couldn't die, I had so much more to achieve. Have I achieved it yet?

SERACH: You still have time.

(METHUSELAH falls onto the floor, having convulsions.)

Thusy? Thusy? Doctor!

(The DOCTOR enters and motions for the HANDMAIDENS to leave. They unfreeze and exit. The DOCTOR examines METHUSELAH.)

DOCTOR: I'm afraid he's taken a turn for the worse.

SERACH: A turn for the worse? What could be worse than having one day left to live?

DOCTOR: Having an hour left.

SERACH: An hour?

DOCTOR: To be precise, fifty-two minutes. And twelve seconds.

SERACH: How miraculous modern science is. To be able to predict the moment of one's death so precisely.

DOCTOR: I am an expert in the field. A mortologist. I can do the same for you, if you'd like.

SERACH: I'd prefer it if you didn't.

DOCTOR: Ah. You like surprises, then?

SERACH: You might get it wrong. I'd hate to have to sue you for malpractice.

DOCTOR: I never get anything wrong. Not when it's within my field.

SERACH: If you're such an expert, why don't you cure him?

DOCTOR: My dear lady, curing the patient is the antithesis of a mortologist's calling. After going through the trouble of the examination, the calibration, the recalibration, and the mortoscopy, and then running all the results through our carefully prepared algorithms and formulae, you can't seriously ask us to sabotage our own findings by throwing a whole new variable in the mix, the variable of the possible cure. It would drive us out of business. As it is we have to deal with such unexpected phenomena as random accidents, like car crashes or miracle cures.

SERACH: How about man's will to survive? Have you accounted for that?

DOCTOR: *(Laughing)* A problem for amateurs alone, I assure you. We are scientists, Madame, not philosophers. Believe what you want to believe, but it will not prevent the sun from setting, the atom from splitting or man's soul from departing his body. And this soul is due to depart in exactly—fifty minutes. And twenty-three seconds.

SERACH: Can't I do anything for him? Please, doctor.

DOCTOR: My dear, why are you so worried? Don't you know what it will mean, when he's dead? You'll be the oldest living human being left. No longer will you have to stand under the shadow of his glory. You'll have glory of your own, fame, notoriety. Why should it be that he gets all the attention, and you get nothing? What is he? A selfish, lecherous old man. There are others who can offer you more. Much more.

SERACH: You perhaps?

DOCTOR: I've seen you looking my way.

SERACH: Perhaps long ago.

DOCTOR: If you looked once, you'll look again.

SERACH: Not if I can help it.

DOCTOR: You'll change your mind eventually. No one can resist the charms of a handsome doctor forever.

SERACH: The answer's no.

DOCTOR: Oh well. It's your funeral.

(The DOCTOR exits.)

METHUSELAH: Serach... Serach...

SERACH: I'm here, darling.

METHUSELAH: You saved me, Serach.

SERACH: I did my best.

METHUSELAH: I'm sorry Serach. I'm sorry I haven't been a better husband.

SERACH: Don't be foolish.

METHUSELAH: I tried. I kept trying. I'm just…a little selfish, that's all.

SERACH: Shhh. You need your rest.

METHUSELAH: How long have we been together now?

SERACH: A long time.

METHUSELAH: Four hundred years in Egypt. I remember that. I didn't even notice you for the first two hundred. I don't know what I was thinking.

SERACH: The same thing we all were thinking about. Food. Water. Freedom. How much time there was till the next break.

METHUSELAH: For two hundred years we slaved together, sometimes even side by side, and I don't think I so much as glanced over once. I was too worried about how I would make it through the next hour, or just the next minute. Funny thing about being a slave. The years pass in an instant, but the days seem to last forever.

SERACH: I noticed you.

METHUSELAH: You did?

SERACH: I didn't like you much at first. But I noticed you.

METHUSELH: You should have said something.

SERACH: I did. It just took you two hundred years to listen. *(The light changes. They are in Egypt.)*

METHUSELAH: Hello, there.

SERACH: Oh. Hello.

METHUSELAH: Looking for some water?

SERACH: Uh, yeah.

METHUSELAH: Here's the well.

SERACH: Thanks. I know.

METHUSELAH: Don't you have a pail?

SERACH: Oh. No. Must have forgotten it. Look, I should go.

METHUSELAH: Wait, don't go.

SERACH: Why not?

METHUSELAH: Haven't I seen you somewhere before?

SERACH: I don't think so.

METHUSELAH: I'm almost sure of it. I never forget a pretty face.

SERACH: Oh, please.

METHUSELAH: Maybe I can walk over to get your pail with you.

SERACH: Come on, Methuselah, do you think there's any slave girl who doesn't know that you hang out by the well, trying to pick up women? Don't you have a pyramid to build?

METHUSELAH: I'm on break.

SERACH: Look, I'll be back later.

METHUSELAH: Wait a second. Wait a second.
SERACH: What?
METHUSELAH: I really have seen you before.
SERACH: No kidding.
METHUSELAH: Serach, isn't it?
SERACH: Listen, Methuselah, this isn't the day for this. Really.
METHUSELAH: It is Serach, isn't it?
SERACH: Yes.
METHUSELAH: I knew it. Didn't you used to play the harp?
SERACH: I used to.
METHUSELAH: How's that going?

(SERACH rubs her hands.)

SERACH: I stopped.
METHUSELAH: What happened?
SERACH: Two hundred years of slavery.

(SERACH turns her head away. She is crying.)

METHUSELAH: Hey. Hey.
SERACH: What?
METHUSELAH: These situations always make me feel kind of awkward.
SERACH: Sorry.

(METHUSELAH goes over and pats her awkwardly on the back.)

METHUSELAH: Things will get better. They always do. Well, sometimes they get worse. Much worse. But then better again.
SERACH: Thanks.
METHUSELAH: Want to have sex?
SERACH: What?
METHUSELAH: It always cheers me up.
SERACH: You've lived thousands of years, and that's your best pick-up line?
METHUSELAH: You know, every hundred years or so, it works. Anyway, it distracted you, didn't it?
SERACH: A bit.
METHUSELAH: How did you know I was so old?

SERACH: Everyone knows. People talk.

METHUSELAH: Well, they're wrong. I'm only nine hundred and sixty-nine.

SERACH: Sorry.

METHUSELAH: Hey, you're pretty old, too, aren't you?

SERACH: You really know how to woo a girl.

METHUSELAH: That harp thing—I saw you perform before we were slaves. It was in Jacob's tent, wasn't it?

SERACH: Yes.

METHUSELAH: That's right. And he blessed you with long life.

SERACH: I don't know about blessed, but yes.

METHUSELAH: Sure, he blessed you. What do you mean? You must have lived for over two hundred years now. That's a blessing.

SERACH: I've lived two hundred years as a slave.

METHUSELAH: Yeah. Bad timing, that.

SERACH: Most people only have to live thirty, forty years this way. Maybe a hundred, if they're particularly unlucky. I've spent two hundred years here and counting. And so have you, I guess. How can you stand it? What prevents you from just throwing yourself down this well?

METHUSELAH: What prevents you?

(SERACH looks away.)

I see. Do you know what you need?

SERACH: What?

METHUSELAH: A vacation.

SERACH: Really? Know any good spots?

METHUSELAH: How about right here, at this well? We'll go on vacation together. We won't go back for an hour. Or two.

SERACH: Do you want to get beaten?

METHUSELAH: I've done it before.

SERACH: And what happened?

METHUSELAH: They beat me.

SEARCH: Was it worth it?

METHUSELAH: They didn't kill me. And it made my life worth living. So yes, it was worth it.

SERACH: I've seen it sometimes. I've seen what they do to people. And...I've experienced it. There's a reason I don't play harp anymore. Last time, they cut my hands so badly...

METHUSELAH: I'm sorry.

SERACH: But you ignore it. Like it doesn't even matter.

METHUSELAH: It matters. It matters a lot. I won't lie to you, it's horrible. But right now, I'm on vacation.

SERACH: All that horror, so you can hang out by the well sometimes and pick up women.

METHUSELAH: You say that as if it's insignificant.

SERACH: Well, it is.

METHUSELAH: Not to me. I'm on a quest for love.

SERACH: A quest for love? Are you serious?

METHUSELAH: I don't know. If I say yes, will you have sex with me?

SERACH: No.

METHUSELAH: Will you kiss me, then?

SERACH: Kiss you?

METHUSELAH: It's more fun than throwing yourself down a well.

SERACH: What makes you think I was going to do that?

METHUSELAH: Were you?

SERACH: Yes.

METHUSELAH: Kiss me, instead. Just a little one.

SERACH: Oh, all right.

(They kiss. METHUSELAH starts laughing uproariously. They are old again.)

METHUSELAH: Slipped you a little tongue, didn't I?

SERACH: Oh, Thusy.

METHUSELAH: Played a little tonsil hockey.

SERACH: That's disgusting.

METHUSELAH: I was pretty smooth, wasn't I?

SERACH: Yes. Yes, you were pretty smooth.

METHUSELAH: You weren't really going to throw yourself down that well, were you?

SERACH: Yes, I was.

METHUSELAH: What were you thinking? That thing wasn't deep enough. You wouldn't have killed yourself. You would have broken your legs, at most. Maybe if you went headfirst...

SERACH: Methuselah!

METHUSELAH: What changed your mind? Was it my general sex appeal?

SERACH: You kept me distracted for the next two hundred years. And then...we weren't slaves any more.

METHUSELAH: Plenty of other terrible things happened. Awful, horrible things.

SERACH: You kept me distracted.

(He kisses her on the forehead.)

METHUSELAH: Old bitch. I love you.

SERACH: Thank you. I suppose. I love you, too.

METHUSELAH: I got you into the Bible, too. Slipped the scribe a few shekels, and there you were. Alongside Jacob's fifty-three grandsons, one of his granddaughters.

SERACH: I wish we had been able to get a mention for my sisters, too.

METHUSELAH: I could barely afford you. But we got the most for our money. That scribe didn't know where to put you, in Jacob's time or in the desert, so he threw you in everywhere. Confused everyone.

SERACH: Thank you. It was a wonderful wedding present.

METHUSELAH: I just wish I had picked a better spot for our honeymoon.

SERACH: Pompeii.

METHUSELAH: That was a close one. If not for you... One day, I promise, I'll give you the honeymoon you deserve.

(The sound of waves is heard. METHUSELAH and SERACH are on the beach, in Pompeii.)

SERACH: Are you happy, dear Thusy?

METHUSELAH: Very. I feel like I'm one hundred years old again. Much better then all those years of slavery in Egypt, isn't this?

SERACH: We had plenty of years of slavery right here, too.

METHUSELAH: No. That's not possible.

SERACH: Of course it is. Remember Spartacus?

METHUSELAH: You're right. That old fool. There's no better way to get yourself killed than to lead a revolution, I told him. He called me a coward. Said I was concerned about nothing but my own life. Or was it Moses who said that?

SERACH: You see, you get them all mixed up. One moment you're talking about the Pharaoh, then the next minute it's about Alexander the Great. It's like your life is just one long story, repeated over and over, just with different actors.

METHUSELAH: Isn't it like that for you?

SERACH: A bit. Sometimes. But at least I can keep straight who is who. You never remember anything quite right.

METHUSELAH: Do you think I'm getting senile?

SERACH: You've always been this way, ever since I met you.

METHUSELAH: It's a slow process, senility. It can last a lifetime.

(There is a rumbling in the distance.)

What's that?

SERACH: That's just thunder. Don't worry about it.

METHUSELAH: What do you mean, don't worry about it? If it rains, how am I going to enjoy my day on the beach?

(The DOCTOR enters.)

DOCTOR: The end of the world is near!

METHUSELAH: God, not him again.

DOCTOR: The gods are angry. The end of the world is near!

METHUSELAH: I've been hearing people say that all my life, and they've only been right once. Or at the most, twice.

DOCTOR: Do not scoff, unbeliever. We live at a time of decadence. The gods have already warned us by shaking the earth two times. I have just come back from the oracle at Delphi, and I assure you, the end of the world is nigh at hand.

SERACH: Delphi was in Greece, dear. Pompeii was in Rome.

METHUSELAH: Well, he had come from some oracle or other, I remember that.

DOCTOR: Oh, great Zeus—

SERACH: Jupiter.

DOCTOR: Great Jupiter, take pity on these lowly mortals, for they know not what they do.

SERACH: I don't think he said—

METHUSELAH: I renounce this city, its sins, and everything within it! *(Pause)* Nothing.

SERACH: I thought you didn't believe him.

METHUSELAH: I don't. But you can never be too careful.

DOCTOR: The great gods have proclaimed—

METHUSELAH: All right, all right, we heard you. Now go away and preach to someone else. Don't you see we're trying to enjoy a relaxed day on the beach?

DOCTOR: Woe befall unto you, scoffer. I see your end. It is written in the stars.

(Another rumble is heard.)

The gods themselves speak against you.

METHUSELAH: It wouldn't be the first time.

SERACH: Come on, Thusy, dear, lets go back to the city. We'll be safe form the rain there.

(METHUSELAH and SERACH get ready to leave.)

METHUSELAH: What is this new Thusy thing of yours? What makes you start calling me Thusy, all of a sudden?

DOCTOR: You cannot escape the wrath of the gods!

METHUSELAH: Listen to him, it's pathetic. Anything for a little attention.

(The HANDMAIDENS enter, carrying trays full of food.)

Now, this is more like it. No one gave feasts like the Romans, I must say. Can we have a bunch of grapes here? *(HANDMAIDEN 1 brings him grapes.)*

SERACH: I am not going to do this again.

METHUSELAH: Come on, just once, it'll be fun.

SERACH: Eat the grapes yourself.

METHUSELAH: Please.

(SERACH sighs and takes the grapes. METHUSELAH leans back across her lap, as she hangs the grapes above his head, feeding them to him.)

SERACH: This is only fun for one of us.

METHUSELAH: Now a little wine.

(HANDMAIDEN 2 brings wine, in a bladder. He lets it pour like a stream into his mouth.)

SERACH: You're going to end up in the vomitorium again.

DOCTOR: Avoid alcohol. Avoid grapes. Avoid salts, cholesterol, red meats, saturated fats, unsaturated fats, barbecued food, fried foods, carbohydrates, preservatives, egg yolks, egg whites, mad cows, sane cows, confused cows, bulls, the other white meat, the other red meat, all meat, fifty times your body weight in any vegetable, fruit, fish, bread, water, orgiastic feasts that require multiple acts of enforced regurgitation followed by further periods of uncontrolled binging—

METHUSELAH: More, more, give me more!

DOCTOR: If it feels good, don't do it.

SERACH: I think you've had enough, dear. You'll be up all night, as it is.

METHUSELAH: Then bring on the dancing girls!

(Music comes on, and the HANDMAIDENS drop their trays. They begin a dance that resembles a belly dance. They swirl their abdomens alluringly, but there is a crashing sound and one drops to the floor, continuing to belly dance there. There is another crashing sound, and the other does the same. Suddenly, it doesn't seem quite as if they're doing a sexual dance anymore, it seemed as if they're crawling desperately towards an exit. The music

takes on an ominous sound. The struggle gets more desperate, and the HANDMAIDENS become more tired. METHUSELAH rushes forward.)

METHUSELAH: What's wrong? Somebody help them, please help them.

DOCTOR: The gods are angry! The gods are angry!

(The DOCTOR rushes from the stage. The rumbling sound returns, and yells are heard. METHUSELAH tries to drag one of the HANDMAIDENS off with him, but falls coughing to the ground himself.)

SERACH: Thusy! Thusy!

METHUSELAH: This is it, I'm afraid. I don't even think I'll last that last forty minutes, or however long that damn doctor says I have. It's those damn poisonous fumes. You always think of it being the lava, but it's those fumes that really get you.

SERACH: Take my arm, Thusy!

METHUSELAH: No, run. Save yourself.

SERACH: Take my arm!

METHUSELAH: The handmaidens...

SERACH: It's too late for them.

(SERACH picks up METHUSELAH and drags him away. He looks back.)

METHUSELAH: The whole city was covered in lava. If we hadn't left just when we did, we would never have escaped.

SERACH: Then it's lucky we left.

METHUSELAH: But how did we escape, even so? You can't outrun an erupting volcano.

SERACH: I just ran, with you. All I knew is I had to save you.

METHUSELAH: A whole city. Frozen in place for nearly two thousand years, until they could be found and analyzed. This man was a priest, this man an actor, this man a gladiator, in the arena when Vesuvius erupted. The lava hit so quickly, his arm was frozen in mid-swing. A museum of Roman life.

SERACH: But we survived. That's what's important.
METHUSELAH: Why did it happen? Weren't there ten good men in Pompeii?
SERACH: You're thinking of Sodom and Gomorrah. You're mixing things up again.
METHUSELAH: That doctor was right. The gods were angry.
SERACH: Not the gods. It was just a fault line, pressure from below the earth.
METHUSELAH: The god of the underworld, then. Pluto.
SERACH: It was nature.
METHUSELAH: What's the difference?
SERACH: You can appease the gods.
HANDMAIDEN 1: Methuselah...
METHUSELAH: We could have saved her! I knew we could have saved her! You should have let me.
SERACH: I could barely drag you. I would never have dragged both of you.
HANDMAIDEN 2: Methuselah...
METHUSELAH: Listen to her! We should have tried.
SERACH: You just think they were alive. You just believe it.
METHUSELAH: No. I could swear. When we left, I saw one of them breathe. I forget which one. But, as you dragged me away, I saw a chest rise and fall. And I thought, save myself. Once again, I thought, save myself. I could have cried out. I could have said something.
SERACH: I wouldn't have listened.
METHUSELAH: You stopped and waited for me. You risked your life for me. I risk my life for no one. That's all I care about, my life. As long as I live, everyone else can die. Including you.
SERACH: That's why you're the oldest man on earth.
METHUSELAH: And the wickedest.
SERACH: And the most virtuous.
METHUSELAH: You just say that because you love me.
SERACH: I love you because it is true.

(The DOCTOR enters.)

DOCTOR: The end of the world is near, Methuselah.

METHUSELAH: You've said that before.

DOCTOR: And I've been right. It's a point of pride, in my profession. The end of the world is at hand. I have examined the world, and it is sick at its very core. It believes itself to be immortal. It is a form of insanity.

METHUSELAH: Then the choice is to be mad or suicidal.

DOCTOR: Not true. If that were true, I'd never have any patients. The sane man fights against death. I have the doctor's bills to prove it.

METHUSELAH: But he loses.

DOCTOR: Inevitably.

METHUSELAH: And that is sanity? To bet on a losing horse in a fixed race? To wage war on a foe you have no hope of defeating?

DOCTOR: Paying the doctor's bills, drinking the medicine, going on diets, exercise programs, invasive procedures, chemotherapy, aromatherapy, psychotherapy, life support, cryogenics. The joy is in the struggle.

METHUSELAH: Is all that really as fun as it sounds?

DOCTOR: Sometimes things get less pleasant.

METHUSELAH: I know. I've seen it.

SERACH: Don't, Thusy...

METHUSELAH: I've seen it get *much* less pleasant.

SERACH: You get too upset.

(The DOCTOR motions, and the HANDMAIDENS stagger to their feet, take hands, and circle)

HANDMAIDENS: Ring around the nosie
Pocket full of posy
Ashes, ashes,
All fall down.

(They collapse. The DOCTOR takes out a makeup stick and draws a black ring around METHUSELAH's nose. METHUSELAH starts coughing violently. He puts a hand to his mouth.)

METHUSELAH: Blood.
DOCTOR: The beginning of the end.
METHUSELAH: The stuff of life.

(The DOCTOR draws a ring around SERACH's nose. SERACH starts coughing.)

DOCTOR: This was my favorite time of history.

(SERACH walks towards the DOCTOR.)

SERACH: Doctor, doctor, please tell where we might find a cure...

DOCTOR: Get away from me. Get away from me. Plague! Plague!

(The DOCTOR runs off. SERACH staggers toward the HANDMAIDENS. They scream and run off. METHUSELAH is overcome by a fit of coughing.)

SERACH: You had better lie down, dear. You're not well.

METHUSELAH: Neither of us are. We both need rest. We both need a cure.

SERACH: The world needs a cure.

METHUSELAH: We just need to search for one. I had heard that someone had found it. The Jews, they say, don't get sick, at all. They say it's because they're in league with Satan.

SERACH: We *are* Jews, Thusy dear.

METHUSELAH: Shhh. Someone will hear. If someone finds out we're in league with Satan, they may alert the church. I don't want to have to deal with the Inquisition, as well as the plague.

SERACH: I'm not in league with Satan.

METHUSELAH: Maybe you haven't tried hard enough. Try to use some of your black arts.

SERACH: I don't know any.

METHUSELAH: Oh mighty Lucifer, I renounce this world, its good deeds, and everything within it. Just save me from the scourge of plague. *(He waits.)* I don't feel much better. Do you feel any better?

SERACH: Why should I? You didn't ask him to save me.

METHUSELAH: I—I forgot.

SERACH: You always forget.

METHUSELAH: Not next time. I promise. Oh mighty Buddha—

SERACH: Will you stop it? That's not going to work. We live in a godless era.

METHUSELAH: How can you say that? Look at what's happened to the world. Somebody has to be responsible.

SERACH: It's overpopulation. Ignorance. Bad hygiene.

(SERACH coughs.)

METHUSELAH: I will find us a cure, my love. There's always a cure.

SERACH: Don't leave me. If we're going to die, we should die together.

METHUSELAH: I'm not going to die.

(METHUSELAH leaves SERACH. He sees the DOCTOR enter, dragging in HANDMAIDEN 1. She has a black circle around her nose.)

HANDMAIDEN 1: Will this really cure me?

DOCTOR: How much gold do you have?

(HANDMAIDEN 1 pulls out a sack of gold.)

This will cure you.

(The DOCTOR hands her a bottle of medicine. It bears a large skull and crossbones.)

HANDMAIDEN 1: *(Pointing to skull and crossbones)* What does this mean?

DOCTOR: It's my personal trademark. Soon everyone will be familiar with it.

(The DOCTOR leaves HANDMAIDEN 1, heading towards an exit. METHUSELAH stops him.)

METHUSELAH: Give me some, too.

DOCTOR: You? I thought you didn't trust doctors.

METHUSELAH: Please. I need a cure.

DOCTOR: It wouldn't do you any good. Trust me, I made it.

METHUSELAH: I don't believe you.

DOCTOR: Why? You usually refuse to take my drugs. Now, when I won't give them to you, you want them.

METHUSELAH: It may be my only chance. I have to believe it will work.

DOCTOR: I know. Isn't it wonderful? I've been making a killing.

METHUSELAH: Please.

DOCTOR: I'm all out. Sorry. Come back during the next plague. Maybe I'll have made up a new batch.

(The DOCTOR exits. HANDMAIDEN 1 gulps down some medicine, gags on it, and gulps down some more.)

METHUSELAH: What is that?

HANDMAIDEN 1: Get away from me!

METHUSELAH: Can I try some?

HANDMAIDEN 1: Get away!

(HANDMAIDEN 1 is overcome by coughing. SERACH simultaneously coughs, where she is lying. HANDMAIDEN 1 takes another long gulp of the medicine.)

METHUSELAH: Don't drink it all!

HANDMAIDEN 1: Why shouldn't I?

METHUSELAH: You'll...you'll overdose.

HANDMAIDEN 1: The doctor would have warned me of that.

(METHUSELAH stares at her, silently.)

METHUSELAH: Can I have a sip?

HANDMAIDEN 1: No!

METHUSELAH: Just a taste.

HANDMAIDEN 1: Get away!

(HANDMAIDEN 1 and SERACH cough again. HANDMAIDEN 1 takes some more medicine. METHUSELAH looks at the diminishing amount of medicine, worried.)

METHUSELAH: I'll pay you.

HANDMAIDEN 1: I don't need your money.

METHUSELAH: I'll give you anything you want—clothes, food, the secret of immortality.

HANDMAIDEN 1: If you had that, you wouldn't need to come to me for help.

METHUSELAH: That's part of the secret.

(HANDMAIDEN 1 and SERACH cough again, and HANDMAIDEN 1 drinks more. METHUSELAH pulls out a knife.)

Give me that medicine.

HANDMAIDEN 1: Get away! I'll call the police.

METHUSELAH: Nobody will come.

HANDMAIDEN 1: Help! Help!

METHUSELAH: Nobody will get near us. They're afraid of us. They're afraid they'll catch the plague.

HANDMAIDEN 1: Please, don't hurt me.

METHUSELAH: I won't hurt you. Just give me a little of that medicine.

HANDMAIDEN 1: No!

(METHUSELAH jumps on her and wrestles the medicine from her.)

HANDMAIDEN 1: Please, don't drink it. Please!

(METHUSELAH finishes what's left in the bottle, then gags. He puts a hand over his mouth and drags himself offstage. There are sounds that indicate he is retching. The HANDMAIDEN starts coughing, then dies. METHUSELAH crawls back onstage.)

METHUSELAH: I'm sorry. I had to try it. It could have been my only hope.

(METHUSELAH crawls over to HANDMAIDEN 1 and realizes that she's dead.)

Oh my God. Oh my God.

(METHUSELAH is overcome by another fit of coughing. The DOCTOR enters.)

DOCTOR: I told you it wouldn't do you any good.

METHUSELAH: Oh my God.

DOCTOR: It didn't do her any good. Not that she was able to drink the whole prescription. Who knows, that might of saved her.

METHUSELAH: Charlatan!

DOCTOR: Now, now, you have no proof of that. I can't guarantee my remedies, if they are disrupted by the disreputable.

METHUSELAH: She was so beautiful. Some people wouldn't have been able to tell, with the plague. But I could tell.

DOCTOR: Yes, very beautiful. Very beautiful, indeed.

(HANDMAIDEN 1 comes to life, moving lasciviously across the floor.)

Sexy, too, huh? The dead are always a little sexy, don't you think?

METHUSELAH: Stop it! That's not what I meant.

(But he stares at HANDMAIDEN 1, nonetheless. She exits, beckoning to him. He takes a step or two towards her, then stops himself.)

I meant it could have been Serach.

(SERACH coughs again.)

DOCTOR: And how is Serach, these days?

METHUSELAH: I...I don't know. I haven't seen her for a while.

DOCTOR: Maybe I ought to check up on her. I'm sure she needs medical assistance.

METHUSELAH: You stay away from her!

(The DOCTOR exits, walking by SERACH and blowing her a kiss as he does. METHUSELAH is taken over by a fit of coughing. HANDMAIDEN 2 enters.)

METHUSELAH: Your...nose.

(HANDMAIDEN 2 backs up from him.)

HANDMAIDEN 2: What about my nose?

METHUSELAH: It's...there's no ring around it.

HANDMAIDEN 2: I know.

METHUSELAH: How come?

(METHUSELAH approaches her.)

HANDMAIDEN 2: Get away from me!

METHUSELAH: I'm sorry. I know. You're afraid of catching the plague.

HANDMAIDEN 2: That's not it.
METHUSELAH: That's not it?
HANDMAIDEN 2: I'm...immune.
METHUSELAH: Immune? How?

(HANDMAIDEN 2 starts to run away. METHUSELAH grabs her leg and holds on tight, so she can't escape.)

HANDMAIDEN 2: Let me go! Please, let me go!
METHUSELAH: I have to know. How are you immune? Is it a cure? Is it a spell? Is it through the help of Satan?
HANDMAIDEN 2: I am not a witch!
METHUSELAH: Then what?
HANDMAIDEN 2: Please. I haven't harmed anyone.
METHUSELAH: I'm not going to do anything to you. Just tell me. How did you become immune?
HANDMAIDEN 2: You won't believe me.
METHUSELAH: I'll believe anything, right now, if it will cure me.

(HANDMAIDEN 2 takes out a vial.)

HANDMAIDEN 2: It's this.
METHUSELAH: This? But it looks like nothing.
HANDMAIDEN 2: This saved me.
METHUSELAH: I've grown to distrust medicines.
HANDMAIDEN 2: I thought you would believe whatever I told you.
METHUSELAH: Yes. I'm sorry.
HANDMAIDEN 2: Anyway, it's not a medicine, it's the water of life.
METHUSELAH: What's the difference?
HANDMAIDEN 2: Marketing.
METHUSELAH: All right, I'll take it. How much?
HANDMAIDEN 2: It's not for sale.
METHUSELAH: I'll pay any price.
HANDMAIDEN 2: The man who sold it to me made me promise I wouldn't sell it to anyone else. It was a stipulation of my buying it.

METHUSELAH: Who sold it to you?

(The DOCTOR enters, holding out a vial.)

I should have guessed.

DOCTOR: Do you want to buy it?

METHUSELAH: Are you selling?

DOCTOR: For the right price.

METHUSELAH: Which is?

DOCTOR: What do you value most, in the world?

METHUSELAH: My life, of course.

DOCTOR: More than your wife?

(The DOCTOR walks over to SERACH and kisses her hand.)

METHUSELAH: Yes. No. I love them both.

DOCTOR: I will trade you this vial for your wife's life.

METHUSELAH: I can't make that trade.

DOCTOR: It is your only hope.

(The DOCTOR kisses SERACH up her arm. They stare at each other.)

METHUSELAH: Don't look at him! Don't look at him like that!

SERACH: I'm so sick, Thusy. I'm so tired.

(METHUSELAH starts coughing violently, falls to the floor.)

DOCTOR: Maybe my calculations weren't quite right, after all. Maybe you have less time than I thought.

METHUSELAH: Why do you even want to save me? I thought it would mess up your carefully worked out time of death.

DOCTOR: Oh, you'll still die in twenty minutes, even if I give you this vial. But if you don't take the vial, you'll die right now.

(METHUSELAH is gasping desperately for breath.)

SERACH: Take the vial, Thusy!

METHUSELAH: Wait a second, what year is it? Are you asking me this now, or were you asking it then?

DOCTOR: It is your final year. It is the nine hundred and sixty-ninth year of your life.

METHUSELAH: I don't believe in your cures!

DOCTOR: The wonderful thing about my cures is that they work, whether you believe in them or not.

METHUSELAH: I can't do this! I love my wife!

(METHUSELAH can barely breathe at all. He gasps and coughs desperately.)

DOCTOR: Then you will die.

METHUSELAH: Give it to me!

(The DOCTOR gives him the vial. METHUSELAH gulps it down. He recovers, wiping away the ring from his nose. The DOCTOR walks over to SERACH, leans in as if for a kiss, then wipes the ring from around her nose. METHUSELAH rushes to SERACH, in horror. She is still alive.)

METHUSELAH: She's alive. Thank God, she's alive.

DOCTOR: I didn't say she'll die immediately. Just someday.

(The DOCTOR grabs HANDMAIDEN 2, who screams.)

METHUSELAH: Where are you taking her?

DOCTOR: To be hanged. The plague has not even touched her. She must be a witch.

(METHUSELAH lunges after him, but is too late. The DOCTOR and HANDMAIDEN 2 exit. METHUSELAH turns back to SERACH.)

METHUSELAH: I'm so sorry.

SERACH: It's all right. I told you to do it. It's all right.

METHUSELAH: I really do love you.

SERACH: I know.

METHUSELAH: I would never kill anyone.

SERACH: You didn't kill me. I suffered, but I was one of the survivors. I lived through the plague.

METHUSELAH: He said you would die.

SERACH: Someday.

METHUSELAH: I'm so sorry.

SERACH: I forgive you.

METHUSELAH: How can you forgive me? What I did was unforgivable.

SERACH: I forgive you, because I can't not forgive you.

Because it was what I wanted you to do. Because I love you.

METHUSELAH: Because of me, you're going to die.

SERACH: Everyone's going to die, someday.

METHUSELAH: Not me.

SERACH: You're the exception. That's why I told you to take the medicine.

METHUSELAH: What's wrong with you? Don't you have any desires of your own? Don't you want to live as long as I do? Longer than I do? If our roles were reversed, I would be furious. Incensed. I would never be able to look at you again.

SERACH: Then I'm glad our roles weren't reversed.

METHUSELAH: Please, just show some emotion. I want you to. Please. I don't want to just sit here and feel guilty.

SERACH: I am showing an emotion.

METHUSELAH: What? Anger? Disgust? Hate?

SERACH: Listen—I love you.

METHUSELAH: That's the kind of statement that can drive a wedge into any marriage.

SERACH: We've lasted a long time, so far.

METHUSELAH: But why have we? You know, my first wife, she hated me. We would have gotten a divorce, if someone had thought to invent the concept in those days. Oh well, I was young, I was foolish. She called me the most selfish man on earth. Of course, that didn't mean as much then—I mean, how many people could there have been on earth at the time. Fifty? A hundred? I forget. Still, she had a point. When the flood came, I forgot to even wake her up and warn her.

SERACH: That's terrible.

METHUSELAH: You see—I am the most selfish man on earth. You agree.

SERACH: Maybe so. But I still love you. It may be why I love you. In a way, it's part of your genius. There are very few outstanding people in the world. Unique people. Epic people. And you're one of them. You couldn't have achieved what you have without being selfish. Without valuing your life above everything, even your first wife's. Even my own.

METHUSELAH: But who am I? What have I done? If I had died, from that plague, how would have people remembered me?

SERACH: As the oldest living man in history.

METHUSELAH: Is that all?

SERACH: Isn't that enough? Most people aren't remembered, at all.

METHUSELAH: But that...that only means something if I'm the oldest living man. If I'm the oldest dead man, I'm just a dead man. That's no accomplishment. Anyone can die.

SERACH: I will always remember you.

METHUSELAH: Only if you live forever. And I ruined that for you.

SERACH: You are written down in the Bible. Because of you, we both are.

METHUSELAH: Footnotes. Trivia questions. I want to have accomplished something. I want my name to be remembered as one of the greats, the great artists, the great inventors, the great intellectuals. Something. Anything. As long as I go on living, I still have time to become one of those. But what am I if I die? Just one man among the millions who tried to cheat death, but failed.

SERACH: Then you will have to keep on living. Why not? Think of what you've lived through. The Flood. Gomorrah. Pompeii. The Black Plague.

METHUSELAH: Hiroshima. Oh my God. Now I remember. That's where I saw them.

SERACH: No, Thusy, don't, it's not safe for you to remember—

(The stage is suffused with a blinding light, and then there is utter darkness for a second. There is an explosion. The lights

slowly rise. SERACH, METHUSELAH, and the HANDMAIDENS are lying on the ground.)

METHUSELAH: Serach?

SERACH: I can't see. I can't see.

METHUSELAH: Neither can I.

SERACH: I'm here, Methuselah.

METHUSELAH: I hear you. I'm coming.

(METHUSELAH crawls towards SERACH. He stumbles over HANDMAIDEN 1.)

Is this you, Serach?

SERACH: Methuselah?

METHUSELAH: Is this you, I feel?

SERACH: I'm here, Methuselah.

METHUSELAH: Then who's this?

SERACH: Who's who?

METHUSELAH: This woman, here. Who is she?

SERACH: Is she alive?

METHUSELAH: I think so. I don't know. *(He takes her pulse.)* I feel a pulse.

SERACH: Then she's alive.

METHUSELAH: My God!

SERACH: What's wrong?

METHUSELAH: Some of her skin came off in my hand.

SERACH: Oh, my God.

METHUSELAH: I'm beginning to see again.

SERACH: Did you look at the explosion? I think, if you looked at the explosion, you'll be blind forever.

METHUSELAH: Not me. I've seen so many explosions. Explosions, eruptions, fire and brimstone. My eyes have grown used to it. They've developed an immunity to any horror.

SERACH: I'm beginning to see again, too. Maybe it was just the initial shock.

METHUSELAH: Or maybe you're developing an immunity, as well.

(HANDMAIDEN 2 moans.)

SERACH: Is that the woman you're with?

METHUSELAH: No. It's someone else. There must be someone else here, too.

SERACH: Both alive?

METHUSELAH: It's a miracle.

HANDMAIDEN 2: What happened?

METHUSELAH: They dropped the bomb.

HANDMAIDEN 2: A bomb?

METHUSELAH: *The* bomb.

HANDMAIDEN 2: I'm burning. Am I on fire?

METHUSELAH: I don't think so. Where are you?

HANDMAIDEN 2: Put out the fire.

METHUSELAH: I can't put out the fire. I can't see any fire.

(He stumbles in her direction.)

SERACH: Thusy?

METHUSELAH: I'm here. I'm still here.

SERACH: I feel sick.

METHUSELAH: I know. So do I.

HANDMAIDEN 2: Help me. I'm burning.

(METHUSELAH reaches HANDMAIDEN 2. He squints at her till his eyes can begin to focus.)

METHUSELAH: You're beautiful.

HANDMAIDEN 2: I'm covered in fire. I'm covered in burns.

METHUSELAH: The fire is beautiful, too. The burns are beautiful. Bright, red, shining.

HANDMAIDEN 2: You must not be able to see right.

HANDMAIDEN 1: My skin...

METHUSELAH: Is that you speaking, Serach? Is that you who's hurt?

SERACH: No, it's someone else.

METHUSELAH: What can we do for them?

SERACH: What can we do for ourselves?

HANDMAIDEN 1: My skin won't stay on my body. It's falling off.

SERACH: This is horrible. Horrible, horrible.

METHUSELAH: They're both so young. They're both so beautiful.

HANDMAIDEN 1: I'm dying...

METHUSELAH: How does it feel?

HANDMAIDEN 1: Terrible.

METHUSELAH: I know. But in what way terrible?

HANDMAIDEN 2: Wonderful.

METHUSELAH: Wonderful? How can it be wonderful?

HANDMAIDEN 2: No more pain.

METHUSELAH: I know that, but without the pain, if you had never had the pain, would it still be wonderful? If it was peaceful, would it be worth it?

HANDMAIDEN 2: Beautiful death.

METHUSELAH: You must be feverish, deranged. But I wish I could know. I wish I could see it. Because, who knows, maybe you're right. Maybe it is beautiful. Describe it to me. What makes it so beautiful?

SERACH: Leave them alone, Methuselah. We should be helping them, not questioning them.

METHUSELAH: But it's the one thing in life I've never experienced. If I never die, how will I know what it feels like?
(The DOCTOR enters.)

DOCTOR: You'll know soon enough.

METHUSELAH: This is your fault.

DOCTOR: It seems to me like they're beginning to enjoy themselves.

METHUSELAH: They're in torture. Death is their only release.
(The DOCTOR laughs.)
Are you that evil? How can you laugh at them?

DOCTOR: I'm sorry, it just reminds me of this joke. There was this guy who walked around every day moaning "Oh, my feet. Oh, my feet." Finally, his friend asked him, "What do you keep complaining about your feet for?" And the guy told him, "It's because my shoes are two sizes too small."

"Then why don't you buy a bigger pair?" asked the friend. "Because," said the first guy, "it feels so good when I take them off." I expect you get the analogy.

METHUSELAH: No.

DOCTOR: Life is like shoes. Well, tight shoes.

METHUSELAH: And you think you've summed up the human condition, right there? In your one stupid joke? Life is like tight shoes?

DOCTOR: I thought it was rather clever, personally.

METHUSELAH: Yeah. You're one hell of a philosopher. Most mass murderers don't have a good joke that they can use in their defense.

DOCTOR: I'm not a mass murderer. I perform a function. A necessary function.

METHUSELAH: Necessary for whom?

DOCTOR: For the world. I am a relief for the world's illnesses. I am the cure.

METHUSELAH: Life is not all self-inflicted pain.

DOCTOR: Maybe it just applies to the wicked.

METHUSELAH: They're not wicked. They're innocent victims.

DOCTOR: They were part of the country that bombed Pearl Harbor. That helped the Nazis.

METHUSELAH: They stayed home. Took care of their families.

DOCTOR: Marched in parades. Cheered the soldiers.

METHUSELAH: They didn't deserve to die.

DOCTOR: If only there had been ten good men...

METHUSELAH: It's your fault. Goddamn mortologists. Splitting the atom. Why was there so much energy inside the atom? It was a trap. In law, it would be called an attractive nuisance. We could sue.

DOCTOR: Less people died this way. It ended the war.

METHUSELAH: You don't know that. The war might have ended by itself.

DOCTOR: If it had been your choice, you would have dropped the bomb, too. Why risk your own life, the lives of your countrymen, when you know for certain you can end all the killing in one last magnificent binge?

HANDMAIDEN 2: Help me. Please, death, stop the pain.

DOCTOR: Don't tell me you wouldn't have done the same. Look at them. There they are. Your handmaidens. Do you remember where you saw them now, your dream girls? Your fantasies? You never could resist an orgy.

METHUSELAH: No. I don't want to look.

HANDMAIDEN 1: Please. My skin.

DOCTOR: *(Lasciviously)* It feels so hot.

HANDMAIDEN 2: The fire.

DOCTOR: Feel it burn within you.

METHUSELAH: Please. I...couldn't even see what they looked like. They were too burned. They must have been...Japanese, I suppose, but I can imagine them any way that I want to, any way but the way they actually looked....

SERACH: Don't look, Thusy. Pretend that you're blind again.

METHUSELAH: I can't. I can't look away. They're too beautiful. It's too beautiful. And not just beautiful.

DOCTOR: Desirable.

METHUSELAH: Compelling.

HANDMAIDEN 1: Help me! I'm going...

METHUSELAH: Tell me how it feels. What's happening to you? Where are you going?

HANDMAIDEN 2: I'm going...

METHUSELAH: Is it hot? Is it cold? Is there a light? Darkness? A sound? Cries of pain? Beautiful music? Do you see your family? Your friends? God? Satan? Is it heavenly? Please, don't go. Don't go without me.

(The HANDMAIDENS writhe in agony and collapse, dead. Silence. METHUSELAH cries. He looks at DOCTOR.)

You bastard!

DOCTOR: Even good doctors sometimes lose a patient.

(The DOCTOR motions to the HANDMAIDENS. They rise and exit, together. METHUSELAH takes a few steps behind them, watching them longingly.)

METHUSELAH: It was the first time I had ever seen anyone die.

SERACH: How can that be? After all the years you've lived. After all the disasters you've lived through.

METHUSELAH: I was always out of the room somehow. Or struggling for my own survival. Or looking in the wrong direction. I saw them before. I occasionally saw them afterwards. But I never saw them during.

SERACH: It must have been terrible for you.

METHUSELAH: It was—not exactly terrible, it was—I was almost tempted to join them. For the first time in my life, I was almost tempted to give in. The Flood, the Plague—these were minor threats, compared to my desire to throw myself off the same precipice they had just jumped from. I saw the ground far beneath, and I thought, why not take that leap. Why not? I had been holding on for so long. So many years. For the first time, those years weighed on me. For the first time, I saw that jump as a release, not a threat. I wanted to jump. *(Pause)* Yes. It was terrible for me.

SERACH: What kept you alive, then?

METHUSELAH: My own mediocrity. I thought, if I die now, what will I have to show for myself?

(The DOCTOR enters, with the HANDMAIDENS. The HANDMAIDENS wear nurse's hats.)

DOCTOR: Five minutes.

METHUSELAH: And how many seconds?

DOCTOR: Eleven.

METHUSELAH: No. No. I'm going to live. I'm the oldest living man on earth. It even says so, in the Bible. I'm going to live.

(A recording of "It Ain't Necessarily So" plays. The DOCTOR and the HANDMAIDENS lip synch the lyrics. As they sing,

they carry METHUSELAH back onto his bed, into the position he was in when the play began.)

DOCTOR: It ain't necessarily so.

HANDMAIDENS: It ain't necessarily so.

DOCTOR: The things that you're liable
To read in the Bible,
They ain't necessarily so.

METHUSELAH: Goddamn doctors. Always think they know better than anyone.

DOCTOR: Methuselah lived nine hundred years.

HANDMAIDENS: Methuselah lived nine hundred years.

DOCTOR: But who calls that livin'
When no gal would give in
To no man what's nine hundred years.
I'm preaching this sermon to show
It ain't nessa—ain't nessa—ain't nessa—ain't nessa

DOCTOR & HANDMAIDENS: Ain't necessarily so.

(The music ends.)

METHUSELAH: Bastard.

SERACH: Not this again.

METHUSELAH: Who does he think he is?

SERACH: It's just a song.

METHUSELAH: Have we had this conversation before?

SERACH: Hundreds of times.

METHUSELAH: Really?

SERACH: Yes.

(Pause. METHUSELAH starts chuckling.)

METHUSELAH: Old bitch.

SERACH: Please, Thusy, stop calling me that.

METHUSELAH: I'll stop calling you old bitch, when you stop calling me Thusy. *(Pause)* I wish I had my handmaidens here.

SERACH: You never had handmaidens.

METHUSELAH: Somebody had handmaidens, I remember that.

SERACH: It wasn't you.
METHUSELAH: Who was it then?
SERACH: Somebody else.
(Pause)
METHUSELAH: Do you think I'm wicked?
SERACH: I think you're human.
METHUSELAH: That means you think I'm wicked.
SERACH: No. That means I don't think the question means anything, for you.
METHUSELAH: Because I'm wicked.
SERACH: Because you're human.
METHUSELAH: But have I accomplished anything?
SERACH: You're a great man.
METHUSELAH: But a great what? I'm a great what?
SERACH: A great survivor.
(Pause)
METHUSELAH: I wish I could have saved them.
SERACH: I know.
METHUSELAH: They were so beautiful.
SERACH: I know.
METHUSELAH: Maybe, if I die, I'll see them again.
SERACH: Maybe, if you die, you'll never see me again.
METHUSELAH: Do you think so?
SERACH: Maybe.
METHUSELAH: I'd miss you.
SERACH: I know.
METHUSELAH: Then I won't die.
SERACH: Good.
(Pause)
DOCTOR: Nurse, scalpel please.
(HANDMAIDEN 1 gets a scythe for the DOCTOR.)
METHUSELAH: Get away from me. That's no scalpel.
DOCTOR: It's a very specialized instrument. A mortologist's scalpel.
METHUSELAH: It's very large.

DOCTOR: The better to cut you with, my dear.
METHUSELAH: Not yet. I still have time.
DOCTOR: One minute.
METHUSELAH: Don't I get something? A meal, a cigarette, some words.
DOCTOR: Whatever you can fit into that minute.
METHUSELAH: A minute is not long enough. Not after nine hundred and sixty-nine years.
DOCTOR: A minute can last a lifetime.
METHUSELAH: But how long can a lifetime last?
(Pause)
DOCTOR: Thirty seconds.
METHUSELAH: Hold my hand, Serach.
SERACH: I'm holding it already.
METHUSELAH: So you are, so you are.
SERACH: I believe in you. I believe in the Living Methuselah.
METHUSELAH: I wish I had the same confidence in myself.
SERACH: You do.
DOCTOR: Ten.
(The HANDMAIDENS put up ten fingers, bringing one finger down with each second.)
METHUSELAH: Stop the clock!
HANDMAIDENS: Nine...Eight...
METHUSELAH: You can't kill me!
HANDMAIDENS: (*Speaking at the same time as METHUSELAH)* Seven...six...five...four...three...two...
METHUSELAH: *(Sitting up)* I can't be killed! I will never die! I...am...the Living Methuselah!
HANDMAIDENS: One...
(The HANDMAIDENS hold one finger up. METHUSELAH sits behind them, full of life. Blackout.)

A Shylock

Original Production

A Shylock was presented by Untitled Theater Company #61 at Theater 22 in New York City in February 1996. It was directed and designed by Edward Einhorn. It was produced by David A. Einhorn. The cast was as follows:

JACOB....................John Blaylock
LAUNCELOT....................Peter Brown*
HAMLET....................Catherine Dunning
TUBAL....................Martin Epstein
PORTIA....................Dina Ipavic
SHYLOCK....................Daniel Leventritt
ANTONIO....................Wesley Stevens
JESSICA....................Deborah Vaughan

STAGING NOTE: In the original production, the full play took place in Jacob's office, and in each scene theatrical trunks were arranged and decorated to symbolize the various settings. Regardless, each scene should take place in its own world, which reflects the way Shylock is interpreted in that world, such as the Nazi world of Scene One, the Freudian world of Scene Two, etc.

*Peter Brown now performs under the name Peter Bean

A Shylock

Prologue

It is the court scene from The Merchant of Venice. *In the background is the Hotel Shakespeare, where Scene One occurs. The DUKE is addressing SHYLOCK, while ANTONIO and BASSANIO stand witness. They are in tableau. JACOB wanders in, reading a copy of* The Merchant of Venice. *He takes a seat at his desk, half reading aloud the lines preceding the scene. The tableau comes to life (it is based on descriptions of* Merchant *productions in Nazi Germany). SHYLOCK has bright, unkempt red hair and a beard, and he displays a grossly elongated nose. He wears a greasy caftan with a yellow prayer shawl slung round. His foot stamps with rage, he gestures claw-like with his hands, and his voice alternates between bawling and muttering. His movements are like those of a caged animal. He is filled with a horrifying, vindictive glee. Overall, he is the most unpleasant possible stereotype of a Jew, pushed to absurd extremes.*

DUKE: We all expect a gentle answer, Jew.
SHYLOCK: I have possess'd your grace of what I purpose,
And by our holy Sabbath I have sworn
To have the due and forfeit of my bond,
If you deny it, let the danger light
Upon your charter and your city's freedom!
You'll ask me why I rather choose to have
A weight of carrion flesh, than to receive
Three thousand ducats: I'll not answer that!
But to say it is my humor—is it answer'd?
(SHYLOCK cackles.)
What if my house be troubled with a rat,

And I be pleas'd to give ten thousand ducats
To have it ban'd? What, are you answer'd yet?
Some men there are that love not a gaping pig!
Some that are mad when they behold a cat!
And others when the bagpipe sings i'th'nose,
Cannot contain their urine—for affection,
Master of passion, sways it to the mood
Of what it likes or loathes,—now for your answer:
As there is no firm reason to be rend'red
Why he cannot abide a gaping pig,
Why he a harmless necessary cat,
Why he a wauling bagpipe, but of force
Must yield to such inevitable shame,
As to offend himself being offended:
So can I give no reason, nor I will not,
More than a lodg'd hate, and a certain loathing
I bear Antonio, that I follow thus
A losing suit against him!—are you answered?
(They freeze. Blackout.)

Scene One

A hotel lobby. A sign says "Hotel Shakespeare – Venice." JACOB is talking to the CLERK.

JACOB: Buon giorno. Sa dirmi dove Shylock?

CLERK: Scusi, non parlo italiano. Only ingeles.

JACOB: I'm sorry, I thought that—never mind. I'm looking for Shylock. Is he registered here?

CLERK: Is Shylock his family name or his Christian name?

JACOB: I don't know—I think it's his only name.

CLERK: I see. *(She checks.)* No, I don't see anyone registered under that name. Isn't he a Jew?

JACOB: Yes, I believe so.

CLERK: That explains it. We don't allow Jews in this establishment. You'll have to look somewhere else.

JACOB: Oh, I see. Well, can I check in, first? I believe I have a reservation. The name is Jacob...Levy.

(The CLERK checks.)

CLERK: Oh, yes, Dr. Levy. It's a pleasure to have a professor of your status here. One moment, our bellboy will lead you to your room.

(The CLERK rings bell. LAUNCELOT enters.)

Launcelot, please take care of Dr. Levy.

(The CLERK exits.)

JACOB: Launcelot? I don't suppose your full name is Launcelot Gobbo?

LAUNCELOT: That's right. You've heard of me, then? Well, don't believe it. It's all an invention, they're just trying to retract from my character. *(Pause)* What have you heard?

JACOB: That you were once the servant to Shylock.

LAUNCELOT: Nothing about the way I tricked Lorenzo out of fifty ducats and three bottles of his best wine?

JACOB: Is it true?

LAUNCELOT: Well, I don't admit to anything, but Lorenzo—

JACOB: I meant about Shylock.

LAUNCELOT: Oh, that. *(LAUNCELOT looks around furtively.)* It's best not to speak of that.

JACOB: But I'm sure that—

LAUNCELOT: Please don't mention it anymore.

JACOB: You are the same Launcelot Gobbo who later became servant to Bassanio?

LAUNCELOT: Please. You never know who's listening.

(A GUARD enters, escorting a JEW. The GUARD spits in the direction of JACOB and LAUNCELOT. The JEW is played by the same actor and dressed in the same way as SHYLOCK was in the prologue. He also wears an armband with a yellow Jewish star. The JEW growls and struggles with the GUARD.)

JACOB: Is that—?

LAUNCELOT: Be quiet. *(In a loud voice)* It's the Jews who are the rumination of Venice, I tell you. Oh, hello sir. I don't suppose you could spare—

(The GUARD throws him a few coins. The JEW leaps for them and the GUARD has to cuff him back. He and the JEW exit while LAUNCELOT picks up the coins.)

Thank you, sir, thank you. *(To JACOB)* They're always suckers for that.

JACOB: Was that Shylock?

LAUNCELOT: The Jew? No. But he does have the same look of the devil about him, I must admit.

JACOB: Then you did know Shylock.

LAUNCELOT: We had better head over to your room, Dr. Levy.

JACOB: I'll double your tip if you answer me truthfully.

LAUNCELOT: You'll make a Jew of me yet.

JACOB: It looked like you were halfway there, a minute ago, when you were scrambling after those coins.

LAUNCELOT: Well, I couldn't refuse his Christian charity.

(JACOB hands him money.)

JACOB: Tell me about Shylock.

LAUNCELOT: Well, I'll tell you, sir, these Jews may all be devils, but Shylock was the very picture of Lucifer himself, a close relative of the man from Malta who poisoned wells at night. "I have plucked my hair from the inferno's fires," he told me once, "and I have stolen my eyes from its dying ambers." It was true, for his breath smelled of rhinestone, and he would scorch my eyebrows when he muttered the incantations that kept me in his power. And for all his money, it was more than he could afford to keep me in the most tattered of rags and feed me the leanest of meats. Half of his rooms were full, from floor to ceiling, with his ill-gotten wealth, and, though you may have heard, sir, that he only asked for flesh from that merchant Antonio, I tell you that one night he whispered to me that "all my gold is nothing else but transformed Christian blood and bone." It is well that his kind is being separated from polite society nowadays, because he had a most fell influence on me, turning me into a liar and a thief. And though I admit I was once devoted to his daughter, now that I think of it, it may well be that she had too much of his accursed blood, as well. It was she who tempted me into some of my worst offenses.

JACOB: Such as?

LAUNCELOT: I helped mix the blood of Jew and Christian.

(The GUARD walks by again, this time with a JEWESS, who is wearing the same red wig, long nose and yellow armband that the last Jew wore. The GUARD spits towards LAUNCELOT and JACOB. The JEWESS bites at the GUARD, who pushes her to the ground. JACOB rushes to help her up.)

GUARD: Don't touch her.

JACOB: I was just trying to—

GUARD: Don't touch her.

(The GUARD pushes JACOB away, grabs the JEWESS and pulls her up.)

LAUNCELOT: Damn Jews. They ought to all be clustered away.

(The GUARD ignores him. He and the JEWESS exit.)

Are you crazy? You could have had us both killed.

JACOB: How could you have just stood there?

LAUNCELOT: She was just a Jew. What are you so concerned about?

JACOB: You could have helped her.

LAUNCELOT: Like you did?

(Pause)

JACOB: Listen, I need to find Shylock. Where does he live? Can you lead me to him?

LAUNCELOT: Not me. I wouldn't be caught dead. You apparently have no such worries. Listen, if you really want a guide, I'm not the one to ask. This is the only quarter of the city I've ever lived in. You need someone who knows something about the city as a whole.

JACOB: I take it you know someone of that sort.

LAUNCELOT: I'm speaking of Hamlet.

JACOB: The Dane?

LAUNCELOT: The Dame.

(HAMLET enters, Yorick skull in hand. She is a woman.)

JACOB: Good day, sweet prince-ess. Excuse me, I was under the impression that you were a man.

HAMLET: So was I. Apparently, I am merely a woman forced by an oppressive society into thinking she's as a man.

LAUNCELOT: Imagine her surprise when she was changing costumes.

JACOB: What are you doing in Venice?

HAMLET: I've been placed in Paris, Beijing, New Dehli, ancient Rome and a futuristic Manhattan, just to name a few places. Being a woman in Venice is merely my latest incarnation.

JACOB: Can you help me find Shylock?

HAMLET: As I was just explaining, it's all a matter of interpretation.

LAUNCELOT: Of course she can. As you can hear, they've had similar histories. Except for the Jew thing, of course.

HAMLET: What is it that interests you so much about that old Shylock?

JACOB: I received a letter.

(JACOB takes out letter and shows it to HAMLET.)

LAUNCELOT: What does it say?

HAMLET: Words, words, words.

JACOB: I got it a few months ago. It says that Shylock is dying, and that he wishes to leave me some sort of inheritance.

LAUNCELOT: I thought that was only the sort of letter you got after someone dies.

JACOB: So did I. Apparently, there's some sort of legal catch, though...

LAUNCELOT: I thought his daughter was supposed to inherit everything after he dies.

JACOB: Yes, that's it. It seems they've had a falling out.

LAUNCELOT: I would say so, yes.

JACOB: Had you heard he was dying?

HAMLET: With that tribe, I've started to assume it.

JACOB: Anyway, I thought I might try to find out a little about him, before I met him, I mean. I feel a little awkward about it. He is a relative, after all.

LAUNCELOT: A relative?

JACOB: Yes, of course. Why else would I inherit anything from him?

LAUNCELOT: I thought you were related to Antonio or something. I hadn't realized—

(The GUARD enters, heading towards JACOB and LAUNCELOT.)

My advice is, don't struggle.

(The GUARD grabs LAUNCELOT and starts to drag him away.)

What are you doing? I'm no Jew.

GUARD: You fucking gypsies are just as bad.

(They exit.)

JACOB: What happened?

HAMLET: He fell victim to dramatic irony. Trust me. I recognize the symptoms. We ought to leave. Once one goes, the rest start falling pretty quickly.

JACOB: Do you know where Shylock lives?

HAMLET: I know where his daughter lives. I think she may be able to help you out.

JACOB: Then lead the way.

(They exit.)

Scene Two

A study and/or a psychiatrist's office. There is a desk and a couch in the room. A MAID escorts HAMLET and JACOB into the room.

MAID: Miss Jessica should be with you in a few minutes. Please make yourself comfortable while you wait, Dr. Shylock. Excuse me. Dr. Levy.

(She exits. HAMLET lies down on the couch.)

JACOB: Are you sure you should lie down on her couch?

HAMLET: I'm only being polite.

(JACOB sits at desk.)

JACOB: How well do you know Jessica?

HAMLET: I know we are similarly complex.

JACOB: Complex? How do you mean?

HAMLET: Shine the light on this wall.

(JACOB does so. HAMLET creates a shape with her hands, which contains a protruding appendage, suggestive in a Freudian way.)

Is this a dagger I see before me?

(HAMLET continues to manipulate the shadow creature. JESSICA enters. She stops, horrified, when she sees HAMLET'S creation.)

JESSICA: Father!

(HAMLET drops her hands.)

HAMLET: The question I have is am I another Electra or a female Oedipus?

JESSICA: I'm sorry—I thought that...

JACOB: Excuse me. I'm sorry to disturb you. My name is Jacob Levy.

JESSICA: Yes, hello, Dr. Levy.

JACOB: Please, call me Jake. After all, we're cousins. And, of course, you're familiar with Hamlet.

HAMLET: How is it with you, lady?

JESSICA: My maid said that you've come on some matter regarding Shylock. I'm afraid I can't give you any information about him.

JACOB: You are his daughter, aren't you?
JESSICA: I am no longer associated with that tribe.
JACOB: I had heard you are his heir.
JESSICA: Oh, yes. I'm his heir. That's true. Why, has he died?
JACOB: He is dying.
JESSICA: Oh. I'm sorry to hear that.
JACOB: I thought that, since I have never met him, I might visit him while I still have the chance to do so. He sent a letter, saying that he wants to meet me.
HAMLET: Among other information.
JACOB: I thought you might know where to find him.
JESSICA: No. I'm sorry. I haven't seen him since I married Lorenzo.
JACOB: Then I'm sorry to bother you.

(He and HAMLET start to leave.)

JESSICA: I'm not a bad daughter.
JACOB: I never said you were.
JESSICA: I had a difficult childhood.
JACOB: I'm sure you did.
JESSICA: I have dreams about him. Often.
HAMLET: Dreams? What sort of dreams?

(HAMLET leads JESSICA to the couch, then sits behind the desk in the psychiatrist's position. JACOB sits to the side.)

JESSICA: I see him walking on the Rialto. I am young, a girl again, and I am picking flowers. I walk up and give one to him, a rose. He sticks his nose in and sniffs it, but he doesn't like it, it makes him sneeze. He starts sneezing and he can't stop, his nose is too large, everyone is staring at him because he can't stop sneezing, so the only thing for me to do is to fix his nose, cut the end off, and make him a Christian. Like me.
HAMLET: Have you ever had the one where you're trying to rule Denmark, but then you suddenly realize you're stark naked?
JESSICA: You have nightmares, too?

HAMLET: Oh God! I could be bounded in a nutshell and think myself king of infinite space were it not that I have bad dreams.

JACOB: I think that means yes.

HAMLET: Only, with me, it's my uncle that does the cutting.

JESSICA: Well, even with the full nose, my father was a very handsome man. Is a very handsome man, I suppose. Dashing, even. I never knew why an attractive man like my father married such an unexceptional woman as my mother. Then she died, and I had him all to myself. I liked that. He still kept a remembrance of her, a ring. He probably loved it more for its monetary value than its sentimental value. Still, I was happier when it was sold. For a monkey. *(She laughs. SHYLOCK has entered. He is just as handsome as she has described. The only remnant of his last incarnation is a long, phallic nose [perhaps the sort associated with Cyrano]. He is also slightly menacing.)*

SHYLOCK: It was my turquoise. I had it of Leah when I was a bachelor. I would not have given it for a wilderness of monkeys.

JESSICA: In my dreams, I can see him. His friend, Tubal, has told him that I have escaped, more than that, that I have married a Christian. But it is not for me he cries.

SHYLOCK: Why, there, there, there! a diamond gone, cost me two thousand ducats in Frankfort! The curse never fell upon our nation till now; I never felt it till now. Two thousand ducats in that; and other precious, precious jewels. I would my daughter were dead at my foot, and the jewels in her ear! would she were hearsed at my foot, and the ducats in her coffin! No news of them? well, so—and I know not what's spent on the search: why, thou loss upon loss! The thief's gone with so much, and so much to find the thief; and no satisfaction, no revenge: nor no ill luck stirring but what lights on my shoulders, no sighs but of my breathing, no tears but of my shedding.

JESSICA: So magnificent in rage.

(SHYLOCK exits.)

I never imagined that I would remain married to Lorenzo. I just wanted my father to be worried about me for once, instead of his stupid business. But events have a way...

JACOB: So do you love him?

JESSICA: Love?

JACOB: Lorenzo.

JESSICA: Shylock.

HAMLET: Gertrude.

JACOB: Closet.

HAMLET: Closeted.

JESSICA: *(Meaningfully)* Antonio.

HAMLET: *(Equally meaningfully)* Bassanio.

JESSICA: *(Surprised)* Portia.

JACOB: Caskets.

HAMLET: Yorick.

JACOB: Clown.

JESSICA: Launcelot.

JACOB: Bastard.

HAMLET: Son.

JACOB: Daughter.

JESSICA: Ducats.

JACOB: Daughter.

JESSICA: Ducats.

JACOB: Daughter.

JESSICA: Ducats.

HAMLET: Gold.

JESSICA: Lead.

JACOB: Death.

HAMLET: Sleep.

JACOB: Dream.

JESSICA: Nose.

HAMLET: Uncle.

JACOB: King.

HAMLET: Usurper.
JACOB: Usurer.
JESSICA: Jew.
HAMLET: Shylock.
JACOB: Jacob.
(Pause)
JESSICA: Jacob. Where have I heard that name before? Oh, that's right, my father mentioned your staff.
JACOB: I think it's my namesake you're thinking of.
JESSICA: No, it's definitely my father.
(The MAID enters.)
MAID: Can I offer you anything? We have bananas, apples—
JACOB: No thank you.
JESSICA: We're fine, Marie, thank you.
MAID: Very well, ma'am. Oh, ma'am, your husband has come home. Shall I tell him to join you?
JESSICA: There's no need. They're not staying much longer.
MAID: Very well, ma'am.
(The MAID exits. JESSICA sits on JACOB's lap.)
JESSICA: Tell me a story
JACOB: Perhaps it's time to go.
JESSICA: Just one more story before I go to bed.
JACOB: I'm married.
JESSICA: So am I.
HAMLET: Frailty, thy name is woman.
JESSICA: Self-hater.
HAMLET: True.
JESSICA: Come on, now, just one ittle-bittle—
JACOB: No!
JESSICA: It's because you love money more than you love me, isn't it? You have only one daughter and thousands of ducats, but it's the ducats you love.
JACOB: What are you talking about?
JESSICA: Please. I promise I'll be good. Very good.
(JESSICA starts kissing JACOB.)

HAMLET: Jacob? *(No answer)* Okay, that's enough, get thee to a nunnery or something. *(No answer)* Remember, she's a Christian.

(JACOB breaks away from JESSICA.)

JACOB: What does my wife's religion have to do with anything?

HAMLET: I meant Jessica. Is your wife—?

JACOB: I'm sorry, Jessica, I shouldn't have let you do that. I suppose I felt bad for you, I felt that if Shylock had shown you more affection—

JESSICA: Yes, Daddy, show me some affection.

JACOB: Now, please—

(LORENZO enters.)

LORENZO: I'm sorry to interrupt, but I heard we had guests. I am Lorenzo. Jessica's husband.

JACOB: I am pleased to meet you. I am—

LORENZO: I had heard that you were here to find Shylock. I'm afraid we can't help you.

JACOB: I had hoped that—

LORENZO: I suggest that you inquire in the Jewish quarter. I believe he is quite often seen in that area.

JACOB: Do you know where?

LORENZO: I believe he had a friend there. What was his name?

JESSICA: Tubal.

LORENZO: That's right. Tubal. He may be able to help you.

JACOB: Do you know where—?

LORENZO: Look in their gathering place. What is it called?

JESSICA: The synagogue.

LORENZO: Yes. The synagogue. I wish you the best of luck with your search, but we can help you no longer.

JACOB: I understand.

JESSICA: Have a good journey.

HAMLET: We'll tell your father you send him your warmest regards.

(HAMLET and JACOB exit.)

Scene Three

A synagogue, in a state of disrepair. Someone has obviously vandalized it. TUBAL and CHUS are trying to make repairs. Apart from them, a third JEW is silently praying. They all wear a red wig and a long nose, although otherwise they are dressed relatively conservatively. They wear yarmulkes and tallises, and the JEW carries a prayer book. HAMLET and JACOB enter.

HAMLET: In thy orisons be all our sins remembered.
(TUBAL and CHUS look up, startled.)
TUBAL: I'm sorry, I didn't hear you come in.
JACOB: The door was open.
CHUS: It's been removed.
JACOB: What's happened here?
TUBAL: It's our weekly interior decorating project.
CHUS: It directly follows the weekly interior desecrating project.
TUBAL: Not that we mind, of course.
JACOB: Is either of you named Tubal?
(TUBAL and CHUS hesitate.)
TUBAL: I am, why?
JACOB: I've been looking for you. My name is Jacob Levy. I'm a relative of Shylock's.
TUBAL: Why didn't you say so? You had us scared for a moment.
CHUS: Are you a relative, as well, ma'am?
HAMLET: No. All my relatives are villains of a more genteel sort.
CHUS: Shylock is no villain at all.
HAMLET: Then we are certainly unrelated.
TUBAL: Well, it's good to meet you, but, you'll have to excuse us, ma'am, women are not allowed in this section of the synagogue. My friend Chus can show you to the women's section.

HAMLET: I'll wait outside.

CHUS: I'll go with you.

HAMLET: Be sure to tell me everything I miss.

(HAMLET and CHUS exit. TUBAL takes off his red wig and long nose.)

TUBAL: It's a good thing we had these on. Though I get the impression she wouldn't have really cared. After all, you're not wearing a wig at all.

JACOB: Why were you wearing fake wigs and noses?

TUBAL: We have to, by law. Otherwise we might be able to mix into Christian society, unnoticed. As you have, apparently.

JACOB: I think I have diplomatic immunity.

TUBAL: So what brings you here, Yakob?

JACOB: I heard that Shylock is ill.

TUBAL: Again?

JACOB: Has he been ill before?

TUBAL: I have often heard that he is ill. I have yet to hear that he has died.

JACOB: What is usually the matter with him?

TUBAL: Natural causes. There's been a epidemic of that around here, recently.

JACOB: I heard that you're a good friend of his.

TUBAL: That's true.

JACOB: I've never met him. I just recently received a letter from him.

TUBAL: Giving away money, again?

JACOB: Giving away money? That doesn't sound like the person I've been hearing about all day.

TUBAL: Shylock is a very generous man. He has often helped me when I was in financial difficulties.

JACOB: You mean, he's given you loans at low interest?

TUBAL: At no interest. It would be against Talmudic law for him to charge interest to any Jew, even if he wanted to. Which he didn't.

JACOB: But I though he was a moneylender, by profession.

TUBAL: It's another law, like the fake wigs and noses. Though, in this case, they just make it illegal for a Jew to take any other job. And, since it's illegal for a Christian to lend money at interest... But, I'm sorry, I don't want to give you a lecture on law. I'll leave that to Portia.

JACOB: It's all right. You might say lectures are my native medium.

TUBAL: Are you a lawyer?

JACOB: No, a professor.

TUBAL: From your name, I thought you were a priest.

JACOB: Jacob?

TUBAL: Aren't you a Levite? You name is Levy.

JACOB: Oh. Yes, I suppose my ancestors were, way back when.

TUBAL: We could do with another Levite. We're getting short on members. If it weren't for Shylock's generosity, we wouldn't have the funds to keep repairing the schul.

JACOB: Which brings me back to my original question. Why does Shylock want to give me his money? I don't think it's out of pure generosity. After all, we've never met. He has no reason to be generous with me.

TUBAL: No, I agree with you. There's another reason he wants to give you money. He gives away money every time he thinks he's going to die. He doesn't want to leave anything to the good-for-nothing daughter of his. He said Kaddish over her, you know. After she ran off with the sheygets.

JACOB: He really said Kaddish over her? How could he have? No matter what, she is his daughter.

TUBAL: Have you ever met her?

JACOB: She seemed to love him, in her own way.

TUBAL: She stole all his money. She renounced him. And, after all that, she married a Christian.

JACOB: Maybe she loved Lorenzo.

TUBAL: Then I am sorry for her. How any Jew can love someone from a people who have so hated and abused us, throughout history, is beyond me. And Lorenzo is no different. He is just another Jew hater.

JACOB: There are plenty of good Christians, as well.

TUBAL: Look around you, Yakob. Look at the destruction in this synagogue. And this is the least of it. How many pogroms have they had? How many Jews have died? How many years have the Jews survived? It's a miracle that there are any of us left, after the crusades. It won't stop there, either. Someday someone will make a concerted effort, a systematic attempt to kill us all. Even then, if we somehow manage to survive that, too, I bet, within a few years, there will be some schmuck who goes and marries a shiksa.

JACOB: *(Very upset)* The children will be raised Jewish.

(A surprised silence)

TUBAL: You mean Jessica's?

JACOB: Yes. Certainly. Jessica's.

TUBAL: Of course they won't. Why would Lorenzo allow that?

JACOB: No, I—of course they won't.

TUBAL: Is there another problem?

JACOB: No. No problem. But I'm not really interested in talking about Jessica. It's Shylock I'm interested in.

(The praying of the JEW becomes audible.)

TUBAL: What about him?

JACOB: If he is such a reasonable man, why did he try to murder Antonio?

TUBAL: After the years of abuse he lived through, he wanted to strike back.

(The JEW removes his false nose and hair. It is SHYLOCK.)

He made his position quite clear to Antonio, if Antonio had been willing to listen. Antonio came to him, hat in hand, begging for money. Antonio, the holy hater of usury. The same man who made it a point to spit at every moneylender who came by. And since he assumed every Jew was a moneylender, you can imagine the result. But it wasn't beneath him to come begging when he needed some extra ducats. Yes, Shylock made his position quite clear.

SHYLOCK: Signor Antonio, many a time and oft
In the Rialto you have rated me
About my moneys and my usances:
Still have I borne it with a patient shrug;
For sufferance is the badge of all our tribe.
You call me misbeliever, cut throat dog,
And spit upon my Jewish gaberdine,
And all for use of that which is mine own.
Well then, it now appears that you need my help:
Go to, then; you come to me, and you say
"Shylock, we would have your moneys:" you say so;
You, that did void your rheum upon my beard,
And foot me as you would a stranger cur
Over your threshold: moneys is your suit.
What should I say to you? Should I not say
"Hath a dog money? is it possible
A cur can lend three thousand ducats" or
Shall I bend low and in a bondsman's key,
With bated breath and whispering humbleness,
Say this,
"Fair sir, you spit on me Wednesday last;
You spurn'd me such a day; another time
You call'd me dog; and for these courtesies
I'll lend you thus much moneys?"

JACOB: No, this is not the Judaism I know. Real Jews are not venomous and vengeful. This is no more real than the red hair.

TUBAL: This is the version of Shylock we offer. Why do you reject it? Have you ever met him? Have you rejected what other people have told you?

JACOB: I have not necessarily accepted it.

TUBAL: That didn't answer my question. Anyway, you have not listened closely. It is not hate that is behind those words. It is a plea for understanding. Not that it helped. Do you know what Antonio's answer was? "I am as like to call thee so again, to spit on thee again, to spurn thee too." And he is considered the most upstanding resident of our city.

JACOB: But murder—there is no excuse for murder.

TUBAL: You're right.

(SHYLOCK vocalizes, with a "Dai dai dai...")

We have sinned.

(SHYLOCK and TUBAL beat their breasts after each of their lines.)

SHYLOCK: Ashamnu.

TUBAL: We have trespassed.

SHYLOCK: Bagadnu.

TUBAL: We have dealt treacherously.

SHYLOCK: Gazalnu.

TUBAL: We have robbed.

SHYLOCK: Deebarnu doafee.

TUBAL: We have spoken slander.

(SHYLOCK continues to chant the prayer, beating his breast after each sin, as TUBAL responds in Hebrew.)

SHYLOCK and TUBAL: He-eveenu. Vuheershanu. Zadnu. Chamasnu. Tafalnu shekair.

(JACOB joins in.)

ALL: Ya-atsnu ra. Keezavnu. Latsnu. Maradnu. Nee-atsnu. Sararnu. Aveenu. Pashanu. Tsararnu. Keesheenu oaref. Rashanu. Sheechatnu. Tee-avnu. Ta-eenu. Teetanu.

TUBAL: I'm surprised, Yakob. I didn't think you'd join in.

JACOB: I find that prayer...moving, somehow.

(SHYLOCK puts on his hair and exits.)

Where is he going?

TUBAL: It's dangerous for any of us to stay in one place too long, especially the temple. You'd better go, too. Unless you want to stay for services.

JACOB: I'm sorry. I still have to find Shylock. Could you tell me any place to go?

TUBAL: I'd talk to Antonio. He's become sort of his keeper, since the trial.

JACOB: Don't you know anything more specific?

TUBAL: You had better get going. Services are going to start any minute.

JACOB: Well, thank you for your help.

(TUBAL turns around and starts working on the temple repairs again.)

Good luck with the repairs.

TUBAL: For gezunterhaydt.

(JACOB exits.)

Scene Four

The Cafe Venice. ANTONIO is sitting alone, smoking and drinking. A PROLETARIAT is scrubbing the floors. HAMLET and JACOB enter.

JACOB: Are you sure this is the place?
HAMLET: *(To PROLETARIAT)* Two vodkas, straight up. We'll be joining Antonio. And a pack of Camels, unfiltered.
PROLETARIAT: Yes, ma'am, right away.
(She exits.)
JACOB: This is not what I expected.
HAMLET: There are more things on heaven and earth, Horatio, then are dreamt of in your philosophy.
JACOB: Jacob.
HAMLET: Sorry, Jacob.
JACOB: Signor Antonio, let me introduce myself, I am—
ANTONIO: No need for introductions, Comrade Shylock.
HAMLET: No, it's Jacob. I just made a similar mistake.
ANTONIO: Of course. And you are Hamlet. I simply misspoke because the word around town is that you are looking for Shylock. Well, sit down, both of you. Join me for a drink.
JACOB: Thank you.
(The PROLETARIAT enters with the vodkas and the cigarettes, including a new glass of vodka for ANTONIO. HAMLET and JACOB light up cigarettes. JACOB slips the PROLETARIAT a large tip.)
PROLETARIAT: Thank you very much, sir.
(She exits.)
HAMLET: That was quite a lot of money for a couple of cigarettes and some vodka.
JACOB: She looked down on her luck.
HAMLET: From each according to his means.
ANTONIO: Well done, comrade.
JACOB: It was an impulse, not a philosophy.

ANTONIO: It's a start.

(The PROLETARIAT returns and starts scrubbing the floors.)

They have quite a good show they put on, here. My friend, Bassanio, you've probably heard of him, he's going to be reading some poetry.

JACOB: So, you had heard of me before I got here?

ANTONIO: Yes. What's that saying?

HAMLET: The play's the thing? Get thee to a nunnery? Alas, poor Yorick; I knew him, Horatio? I mean, Jacob.

ANTONIO: Oh, yes. Nothing travels faster than bad news.

HAMLET: I can't say that I'm familiar with that one.

JACOB: You think my coming is bad news.

ANTONIO: I did. Though I must say I was impressed by that last gesture—forgive me. I'm afraid I've been feeling rather melancholy. I'm not quite sure why. I didn't mean to be insulting. These moods just hit me, every once in a while.

HAMLET: Really? I have a feeling we're going to be good friends.

(The OWNER enters.)

OWNER: Scrub harder, Sonya. If I find one spot, there will be no food for you again, tonight.

PROLETARIAT: Yes, sir.

OWNER: Ladies and gentlemen, I am proud to present open mike night at the Cafe Venice. Our first performer tonight is a woman whom we affectionately know as Empty Drivel. She will be singing a song called "Fancy Bred."

(EMPTY DRIVEL enters.)

EMPTY DRIVEL: Tell me where is fancy bred,
Or in the heart or in the head?
How begot, how nourished?
Reply, reply.
It is engender'd in the eyes,
With gazing fed: and fancy dies
In the cradle where it lies.

Let us all ring fancy's knell;
I'll begin it,—Ding, dong bell.

EMPTY DRIVEL, OWNER, HAMLET and JACOB: Ding, dong, bell.

(All applaud but ANTONIO and PROLETARIAT. EMPTY DRIVEL exits.)

JACOB: What's wrong? Didn't you enjoy the song?

ANTONIO: It was not true art.

JACOB: I thought it was pretty.

ANTONIO: It served no purpose.

JACOB: Your friend, Bassanio, might disagree with you, there.

ANTONIO: We'll see. I believe he is the next performer.

OWNER: Sonya, why didn't I hear you sing "Ding dong bell," like the rest of us?

PROLETARIAT: I was too tired, sir.

OWNER: You mean you didn't sing it at all?

JACOB: No, she sang it, I heard her.

OWNER: Are you sure?

JACOB: Yes.

OWNER: Well, you're lucky, Sonya, that you have this gentleman to defend you.

HAMLET: Another blow struck...

(BASSANIO enters.)

ANTONIO: Here comes Bassanio.

OWNER: Our next performer prefers the name of History. He will be performing a poem called "Down with the Bourgeoisie."

BASSANIO: Revolt.

This is a poem about a woman named Sonya.
This is a poem about a woman named Sonya who had to scrub floors and wait tables all day long.
This is a poem about an owner who became fat on the labor of a worker named Sonya.
This is a poem about an owner who pretended that he did not have enough money to pay Sonya her wages, but really

had all his money hidden inside a safe in his office.
Sonya, the safe is concealed behind that giant painting of Rockefeller. The combination is 28-16-25.
Revolt.
This is a poem.
Thank you.
(All but JACOB applaud. BASSANIO exits. The PROLETARIAT follows him out.)

JACOB: If there's one thing that wasn't, it's a poem.

ANTONIO: Come on, you can't tell me you disagree with his points.

JACOB: I disagree with his artistry.

ANTONIO: That was true art.

JACOB: I'm sorry. I don't mean to insult your friend. But you can't tell me that you enjoyed that more than the song.

ANTONIO: Much more.

JACOB: Why?

ANTONIO: It was true, what he said about the safe.

JACOB: So?

ANTONIO: True art is always a weapon.

(SHYLOCK enters. He is dressed in rich clothes, the picture of a successful, bloated capitalist. He is a pompous fool.)

OWNER: Our final performer is known as The Capitalist. He will be performing a poem called "The Bond."

SHYLOCK: I'll have my bond; speak not against my bond:
I have sworn an oath that I will have my bond.
Thou call'dst me dog before thou hadst a cause;
But, since I am a dog, beware my fangs:
I'll have my bond; I will not hear thee speak:
I'll have my bond; and therefore speak no more.
I'll not be made a soft and dull-eyed fool,
To shake my head, relent, and sigh, and yield
To Christian intercessors. Follow not;
I'll have no speaking: I will have my bond.

(All applaud. SHYLOCK exits.)

OWNER: Thank you, thank you. That concludes our show for this evening. Once again, I would like to extend a final thank you to all our performers. *(He applauds again.)* Sonya? *(He exits.)*

ANTONIO: Recognize the poem?

JACOB: No. Should I?

ANTONIO: Shylock wrote it.

JACOB: Oh.

HAMLET: It certainly was true art. It cut right to the heart.

ANTONIO: It was typical of Shylock. Always looking at the bottom line.

JACOB: And of you, too, I suppose.

ANTONIO: What do you mean by that?

JACOB: Well, you are known as The Merchant of Venice.

ANTONIO: My commerce was in kindness, for mere pay, so that I might live. Shylock's commerce, like that of any Jew, is in unkindness, sucking as much profit as he can from his victims.

HAMLET: I thought you were the richest man in Venice.

JACOB: Are you?

ANTONIO: Well, I'm not sure about that...

HAMLET: Then who is?

ANTONIO: Well, Bassanio's almost as rich as I am. At least, he is when you combine his wealth with Portia's.

JACOB: Then what's the difference between the two of you and Shylock?

ANTONIO: The difference is, we didn't suck the money out of any poor unfortunates. If it were not for me, many of Shylock's victims would have been ruined by him. Fortunately, I was able to lend them the money they needed to pay him off. At no interest, of course. You should have seen how upset he would become when, on the verge of sinking his teeth into the capital of the poor fool who had gone to him for money, the prize was suddenly snatched away at the last second because I had lent out the money.

Gratis. That was what really infuriated him. I think, if I had exploited the poor the way he had, he could have understood that, forgiven it. But when I didn't, when I just gave away my riches, his whole bloated body, stuffed with the ducats of a thousand unfortunate Venetians, would shake and quiver with rage. That was why Shylock really hated me. That was why he wanted to kill me. I was helping to overthrow his world order.

(A scream is heard. The PROLETARIAT enters, with blood on her hands.)

HAMLET: There you are. Can I have another glass of vodka?

PROLETARIAT: I will no longer serve!

(The PROLETARIAT exits. HAMLET shrugs and pours herself some more vodka.)

ANTONIO: What did I tell you, true art.

JACOB: Did she really...

ANTONIO: Of course.

JACOB: Shouldn't we do something?

ANTONIO: It's too late now. History is taking its course. It was inevitable, from the moment profit was invented.

JACOB: That's ridiculous. That had to do with maltreatment, not profit making. It is very easy for you to condemn businessmen, but some people don't have their money handed to them on a platter.

ANTONIO: Well, of course you don't see what's wrong with it.

JACOB: What do you mean?

ANTONIO: Shylock mentioned some trickery of yours, involving sheep.

HAMLET: You probably shouldn't tell him the story about your brother and the beet soup.

JACOB: I think you're referring to Jacob from the Bible, not me.

ANTONIO: Oh, that thing. I guess your people do need that opiate. Thank God, or my own good sense I should say, that I am not another Shylock, captive to his religion.

JACOB: From what I hear, he's more of a captive to you, nowadays, than he is to his religion.

ANTONIO: What are you talking about?

JACOB: I heard you had become his keeper. In fact, I was going to ask you to help me find him.

ANTONIO: Oh, that's out of the question. I mean, I'd help you if I could, but I can't. I don't think that I've seen him since the trial.

JACOB: You mean, you have no idea where I could find him?

ANTONIO: None at all. Maybe Portia can help you. You should ask her.

JACOB: I should have guessed.

(Sounds of fighting are heard from outside, along with cries of "Down with the Bourgeoisie," "Workers of the world unite," and "The revolution isn't over yet.")

ANTONIO: I see Bassanio has been on tour. I should leave. He needs me. Come with me, Jacob. Forget about Shylock. There may still be a chance for you. A small one, considering, but a chance. At least you felt bad for Sonya.

JACOB: I'm sorry. I have to try to find Portia.

ANTONIO: What about you, Hamlet?

HAMLET: I don't know. Well, no. I think not. Sorry, I'm never good at snap decisions.

ANTONIO: Well, I'm not going to leave them to fight alone.

(ANTONIO exits.)

JACOB: It's almost tempting to follow him.

HAMLET: I thought you disagreed with him.

JACOB: I do. But I envy his surety.

HAMLET: Then what do you want to do now?

JACOB: Find a back door.

(They exit.)

Scene Five

A law court. PORTIA is serving as the judge. She wears a white wig. A PLAINTIFF and a DEFENDANT stand before her. JACOB and HAMLET enter silently and take a seat.

PLAINTIFF: ...and furthermore, your honor, when we were growing up, he used to beat me every day. He used to call me ugly and stupid and mock the way I dressed. Often, he would pull down my pants and ridicule the size of my…genitalia. Why, out of everyone in Venice, did he choose to break into *my* house and steal *my* money? Not just because he is poor now, while I am rich. It is because he hates me, your honor. Why should I have any pity for him? I am glad he's going to jail.

PORTIA: I see. Well, legally, of course, you are in the right, and, according to Venetian law, the penalty for theft is disembowelment by starving rats.

DEFENDENT: My God!

PLAINTIFF: I—are you sure about that? I never heard of that penalty.

PORTIA: But why don't you take the more merciful course? Forgive him, and freely give him the money that he stole.

PLAINTIFF: You want me to give him money?

PORTIA: If the defendant is amenable. Would you like the money sir, or would you prefer disembowelment?

DEFENDENT: I would prefer the money, your honor.

PLAINTIFF: I'm not giving him anything.

PORTIA: Well then, I must rule in your favor. Do you have any rats?

PLAINTIFF: Rats?

PORTIA: Do you?

JACOB: I don't think that's necessary, your honor.

PORTIA: Did I ask for your opinion? Be careful you don't get fined for contempt. Sir, do you?

PLAINTIFF: No. Of course not. No.

PORTIA: I see. Coming to court without rats is a grave offense. But I will be merciful to you both. The defendant will be allowed to work off his debt to you. He will be your food taster. Thus, half of what you eat will be his, to taste. Similarly, he will be allowed to spend half your money, to be sure it isn't counterfeit. Similarly, he will be required to have half of the sexual relations with your wife, to make sure she is not—

PLAINTIFF: Enough. Never mind. He can have the money.

PORTIA: It is too late for that. I have given my judgment.

PLAINTIFF: Have a little mercy, for God's sake.

PORTIA: Very well. Your relations with your wife are your own. Are you content?

PLAINTIFF: I am…content.

(The PLAINTIFF leaves.)

DEFENDENT: Thanks.

PORTIA: Are you still joining us for dinner tomorrow night?

DEFENDENT: Of course. See you then.

(The DEFENDANT exits.)

JACOB: You knew him?

PORTIA: Excuse me, but who are you to be questioning me in my court?

JACOB: Well, I know it may not be my place—

PORTIA: It's not.

JACOB: You just seemed a bit harsh with the plaintiff.

PORTIA: How unfortunate for you, then, that I will be judging your case.

JACOB: Oh, we're not here on a matter of law. We're here to see Portia. We were told she might be in this court. Is she on your docket for the day?

PORTIA: I am Portia.

JACOB: But we were told that the judge is a man named Bellario.

PORTIA: *(Uncomfortably)* He was sick. I'm filling in.

(She removes her wig.)

JACOB: Are you sure this is legal? I didn't know women were even allowed to be judges in Venice.

PORTIA: I didn't think women were allowed to dress up as the Prince of Denmark.

HAMLET: It's kind of a complicated issue.

PORTIA: Same here.

JACOB: I see that you are familiar with Hamlet. Let me introduce myself. I'm—

PORTIA: Shylock. How could I have failed to recognize you?

JACOB: Jacob Levy.

PORTIA: That's right. Of course. I don't know what I was thinking. I remember hearing about you. I had Launcelot's trial earlier today.

JACOB: Really? What was the verdict?

PORTIA: He was convicted of consorting with Jews.

JACOB: Which brings us to our previous subject.

PORTIA: Shylock. Interesting case, really. If not for my intervention, Antonio would have been—

HAMLET: Dead, for a ducat, dead. Yes, we've heard.

PORTIA: Shylock was a stickler for the letter of the law. And to tell the truth, he did have that on his side.

JACOB: Actually, I'm not so sure of that. That whole pound of flesh contract seems like it would have been prima facie invalid. First of all, from what I've heard, Shylock pretended it was all a joke. Isn't that called fraudulent misrepresentation or something?

PORTIA: Is it? I'm not familiar with the term.

JACOB: Besides which, how can any contract demanding the slaughter of one of the parties be called valid. If it weren't written as a joke, it would be clear that Antonio wasn't of sound mind when he wrote it.

PORTIA: That's why you reminded me of Shylock. Really, you're a lot like him. Who cares if he pretended it was a joke? It certainly wasn't a joke in the end.

JACOB: If he pretended it was a joke, that would have been—

PORTIA: Habeas corpus? In logo parentis? Or cogito ergo sum? For God's sake, the two of you make it seem as if the law was some foreign language that you have to devote your life to learning before you can even hope to comprehend it. How can we expect lay people to follow the law if we can barely follow it ourselves? The law isn't mumblety-jumblety doublespeak, it's the codification of common sense, tempered by understanding. "Objection, your honor." I can just see Shylock, striding up and down the court, a very serious, scholarly expression on his face while he spouted out his legal treatise on judgment, sounding just like you did when you were holding forth about "fraudulent misrepresentation."

(SHYLOCK enters and takes the stand. He is dressed in a conservative suit. Otherwise, he matches Portia's description.)

SHYLOCK: What judgment should I dread, doing no wrong?
You have among you many a purchased slave,
Which, like your asses and your dogs and mules,
You use in abject and in slavish parts,
Because you bought them: shall I say to you,
Let them be free, marry them to your heirs?
Why sweat they under burdens? Let their beds
Be made as soft as yours, and let their palates
Be seasoned with such viands? You will answer,
"The slaves are ours." So do I answer you:
The pound of flesh, which I demand of him,
Is dearly bought: 'tis mine and I will have it.
If you deny me, fie upon your law!
There is no force in the decrees of Venice.
I stand for judgment: answer, shall I have it?

PORTIA: What about mercy?

SHYLOCK: I crave the law.

PORTIA: What about forgiveness?

SHYLOCK: I stand here for law.

PORTIA: What about goodness, love, compassion? What about doing not what's written, but what's right?

SHYLOCK: I stand for judgment: answer, shall I have it?

PORTIA: Thank you. You may step down.

(SHYLOCK exits.)

You see? He stands for judgment. Well, what would you expect, he's a Jew, his god is an angry god. However, I'm a Christian, and my god is merciful.

JACOB: That's right. How can you call yourself merciful, when you ordered that Shylock be forcibly converted?

PORTIA: What could be more merciful? I saved him from eternal damnation. Well, I tried to, at least. Unfortunately, the conversion didn't really seem to take.

JACOB: What do you mean?

PORTIA: Well, he still seems to wear his prayer shawl and visit the synagogue, when I'm not looking. I don't understand it. I mean, he was baptized.

HAMLET: You can lead a Jew to water...

PORTIA: I should never have let him keep his precious money. I wanted to be merciful, but the only way to truly convert a Jew is to take away the tricks of his trade.

JACOB: It wasn't you who showed him that mercy, it was Antonio. And Shylock showed Antonio mercy, too.

PORTIA: What possible mercy did Shylock show Antonio?

JACOB: He never took his pound of flesh.

PORTIA: Of course he didn't. He had to let Antonio go. He might have been hanged, otherwise.

HAMLET: Actually, I believe the law you quoted was that his goods would be confiscate.

JACOB: Which they were anyway, for attempted murder. In any event, Shylock could easily have followed your stipulations, if he had wanted to. All he would have needed was a very hot knife, hot enough to sear the skin so there was no blood loss. Then he could have cut millimeter by millimeter, until he had exactly one pound.

PORTIA: Shylock obviously wasn't as conversant in these things as you are. Have you had some prior experience?

JACOB: My uncle was a butcher.

HAMLET: I know the feeling.

JACOB: The point is, it could have been done.

PORTIA: The point is, if he had done so, the Duke would have surely condemned him to death. If there is one thing I have learned in all my years of being a judge, it is that a man who hones his knife in court does not usually act out of mercy.

HAMLET: I would imagine that was your first lesson.

(BELLARIO enters, half undressed and with his hands still tied behind his back.)

PORTIA: Signor Bellario, what a surprise to see you in court, today.

BELLARIO: I'll bet it is.

JACOB: Bellario? Aren't you the judge?

BELLARIO: When I can get to court without being abducted. I made the mistake of letting Portia play judge one day, and I'm afraid it's become something of an addiction. So, what illegal judgments have you made today that I will have to reverse tomorrow?

JACOB: Was the judgment against Shylock illegal?

BELLARIO: Shylock? Not that name again. Yes, of course it was illegal. Only the old fool doesn't know it. And, in that matter, I don't know why I should tell him.

PORTIA: Watch what you're saying, for God's sake.

BELLARIO: Why, what lies have you been telling this man? You know, she can be incredibly sadistic. In that Shylock case, for example, she let the Jew almost put his knife against Antonio's breast before she revealed her plan. And I see that she has a new accomplice this time. Madame, I am not fooled by your breeches and tunic. Women are not fit to play men's parts.

HAMLET: Sir, I have been panned by bigger critics than you.

JACOB: How else did she lead people on, in that Antonio case?

BELLARIO: God, I don't know, it was years ago. A thousand different ways. She told Shylock she would rule in his favor, encouraging the lawsuit, when she knew she would rule against him and pretended that she wanted him to drop the suit. And then, I remember, she played this horrible practical joke on her fiancé. Something about engagement rings. She used more cunning than a Jew.

PORTIA: I did a better job of meting out mercy than you ever have.

BELLARIO: Then you should start abducting priests, instead of judges. You notice the phrase is justice of the peace. There's no mention of mercy. Not that you exactly limit yourself to being judge, either. You're usually prosecutor, judge and jury all at once, in a court that switches from civil to criminal and back.

PORTIA: Now you sound like a Jew. Do you, too, crave the law? The important thing is that, in the end, I do the right thing.

BELLARIO: How dare you insult me like that? Get out of my court.

PORTIA: Certainly. I've tried my last case today, anyway.

JACOB: Wait! Before you go, tell me where Shylock is.

PORTIA: I don't remember.

BELLARIO: What do you mean you don't remember? He lives right around the corner.

PORTIA: Oh, Jesus. This is Jacob. Jacob Levy.

BELLARIO: Oh, Jacob Levy.

JACOB: What do you mean, "Oh, Jacob Levy?" Have you been giving me the runaround?

PORTIA: Why don't you ask Bellario. It's his court.

(PORTIA exits.)

JACOB: Well?

BELLARIO: I'm sorry. I have to go. Court has been adjourned.

(BELLARIO exits.)

JACOB: So, one second, when everyone kept telling me that they didn't know where Shylock was, those were all lies?

HAMLET: False as dicers' oaths.

JACOB: Why were they lying?

HAMLET: They wanted to keep their own vision of who Shylock is.

JACOB: And what about you? Have you really known where he is?

HAMLET: No. I am interested in finding out who Shylock is as you were. In fact, I was hoping someone would know who Hamlet is. But I do have my own ideas, that don't necessarily fit with the others.

JACOB: What are they?

HAMLET: I'll show you.

(They exit.)

Scene Six

An empty stage. Caskets are stacked all around. HAMLET and JACOB enter.

JACOB: This doesn't seem like much of a home.
HAMLET: This is it, nonetheless.
JACOB: What are all the caskets for?
HAMLET: They're where he keeps his costumes.
JACOB: How do you know?
HAMLET: I have a similar home, myself. I'm not always a woman, you know.
JACOB: That's not exactly a costume.
HAMLET: It can be.
(She opens a casket and pulls out fake breasts and a dress.)
You see.
JACOB: But you're not—
HAMLET: No. I'm the genuine article. This time.
(JACOB examines a casket.)
JACOB: "All that glitters is gold." What do these inscriptions mean?
HAMLET: They tell what's inside. That one you're looking at is Antonio's favorite.
JACOB: Which one is your favorite?
HAMLET: This one.
(She drags out a lead casket. JACOB examines it.)
JACOB: "This is the Jew that Shakespeare drew."
HAMLET: Actually, it's more like the Jew as the Elizabethans saw him. But that doesn't rhyme, of course. *(HAMLET spots something offstage.)* As you can see for yourself.
JACOB: What do you mean? I don't see him.
HAMLET: May I present to you, Shylock.
(HAMLET points in JACOB'S direction.)
JACOB: I knew it. I knew that was going to be the answer. I am not Shylock.

(SHYLOCK enters from behind JACOB, dressed in his costume from the PORTIA scene, and heads over to a casket, where he removes and deposits the costume.)

HAMLET: Why do plays always bring out a guilty conscience? I never said you were.

JACOB: Oh. It's just that, with all the people who mistook me for him, I thought that, perhaps...

HAMLET: I could always tell the difference. I have a nose for these things. For one thing, you never even changed costumes.

JACOB: *(Hesitantly)* It seems to be Shylock, but...

HAMLET: Seems? I know not seems. It is.

JACOB: Well, you are my guide.

(JACOB hesitantly approaches SHYLOCK, but HAMLET restrains him.)

HAMLET: Wait a moment. Don't talk to him yet.

JACOB: Why?

HAMLET: I want you to see my Shylock.

(She opens the lead casket, and SHYLOCK removes clothes from it and starts putting them on. All his clothes look like they don't quite belong in our world. This might include a version of his yarmulke and gabardine, clown hair, and Ferengi ears, among other possibilities, and should definitely include a set of horns.)

As I see it, the Jew that Shakespeare drew is not a Jew at all. Shakespeare may never have met a Jew in his life. Almost nobody did, in Shakespeare's England. They had been outlawed for such a long time that they had become legendary monsters, boogey men that parents would scare their children with at night, little green men. "Better go to sleep, or the Jew will come and eat you." That's why it was such a common misconception that Jews had horns, like Michelangelo's Moses. So the problem of how Shylock can be so comic while being so tragic is not a problem at all. The assumption that you make is that he was seen as a human being. He wasn't seen as a human being, he was a theatrical conceit, who would count his money and talk about his laws of acquisition. Human beings can be tragic. But a funny alien is always a funny alien.

(HAMLET turns to SHYLOCK.)

0 villain, villain, smiling damned villain!
My tables—meet it is I set it down,
That one may smile, and smile, and be a villain.
At least I am sure it may be so in Denmark.

(SHYLOCK steps forward, presenting himself in his new incarnation. HAMLET takes on another voice, prompting him.)

Why, I am sure, if he forfeit, thou wilt not take his flesh. What's that good for?

(When SHYLOCK speaks, it should be with an unnatural, not quite human voice, possibly very high-pitched, thus putting some doubt on his claims of humanity. He should sound somewhat like a cartoon.)

SHYLOCK: To bait fish withal. If it will feed nothing else, it will feed my revenge. He hath disgraced me, and hind'red me half a million; laughed at my losses, mocked at my gains, scorned my nation, thwarted my bargains, cooled my friends, heated my enemies—and what's his reason? I am a Jew. Hath not a Jew eyes? Hath not a Jew hands, organs, dimensions, senses, affections, passions? Fed with the same food, hurt with the same weapons, subject to the same diseases, healed by the same means, warmed and cooled by the same winter and summer as a Christian is? If you prick us, do we not bleed? If you tickle us, do we not laugh? If you poison us, do we not die? And if you wrong us, shall we not revenge? If we are like you in the rest, we will resemble you in that. If a Jew wrong a Christian, what is his humility? Revenge. If a Christian wrong a Jew, what should his sufferance be by Christian example? Why, revenge. The villainy you teach me I will execute, and it shall go hard but I will better the instruction.

(SHYLOCK bows to the sound of roaring laughter and HAMLET's applause.)

JACOB: What was that?

HAMLET: I just told you. That was Shylock, as the Elizabethans saw him.

(Cries of "Encore, encore." SHYLOCK freezes.)

JACOB: Are you sure that that's really Shylock?

HAMLET: It's as good a guess as any.

JACOB: Then you're not sure.

HAMLET: I'm not even sure who I really am. I certainly make no promises about Shylock. But speaking as an Elizabethan, or at least an Elizabethan character, this is my educated guess.

JACOB: I have never seen him that way. I don't think he was ever performed that way.

HAMLET: I don't care how he was performed. If you, too, were an Elizabethan, this is the way you'd view him.

JACOB: But I am not an Elizabethan. So I view him otherwise.

HAMLET: How is that?

JACOB: I don't know yet.

HAMLET: I'd be interested.

JACOB: Well, I only just met him.

HAMLET: And you want to be formally introduced. I'm sorry. Let me accommodate you. Signor Shylock—

(SHYLOCK relaxes into a normal posture, turning to meet JACOB. Suddenly, JACOB backs away.)

JACOB: Well, maybe you can tell me more about your ideas about his not being a Jew.

HAMLET: You just heard them.

JACOB: I'm sure you could expand on it. I mean, I want to be fully informed when I meet him.

HAMLET: You are.

JACOB: But surely—

HAMLET: Do you want to meet him or not?

JACOB: Yes. Of course I do. Why do you think I came to Venice?

HAMLET: Good. Signor Shylock, may I present to you Dr. Jacob Levy.

(JACOB offers his hand. SHYLOCK looks at HAMLET, pointedly.)

I will leave you two to talk.

(HAMLET hides behind the curtain, then sticks her head out.)

If you have anything sharp, try not to wave it around too much.

(HAMLET returns behind the curtain.)

JACOB: Shylock? *(SHYLOCK is silent.)* It's okay. You can speak to me. I'm M.O.T. *(Silence)* You know…member of the tribe? *(Still nothing)* Listen, I haven't come all this way to be stonewalled. I'm a relative of yours. Remember, you sent me a letter. You said you were dying. Something about an inheritance. You don't have to worry about that, by the way, I just wanted to meet you, anyway. I must say, you look—healthy. How are you feeling? *(Still nothing)* Listen, you are Shylock, aren't you?

SHYLOCK: Shylock is my name.

JACOB: Good. I was beginning to get worried, for a minute, there. Listen, Shylock, I need to talk to you. I know you don't really know me that well, but—

SHYLOCK: *(Still in his inhuman manner)* Hath not a Jew eyes? Scratch us, do we not—

JACOB: Wait, wait, stop all that. I heard it, I know. That's part of what I wanted to ask you about. This, this isn't you. I don't care what Hamlet says, whatever else is true about you, you are a Jew. Speak to me as yourself.

SHYLOCK: *(In a stereotypically homosexual manner)* Hath not a Jew eyes? Scratch us—

JACOB: No!

SHYLOCK: *(With a thick Yiddish accent)* Hath not a Jew eyes—

JACOB: Stop!

(SHYLOCK is silent.)

JACOB: Don't you have any voice of your own? You must. You are not an amorphous collection of other people's thoughts, you are something in yourself. You are a symbol. A good symbol, a bad symbol, I don't know. But if you ask an average person in this world who was the most famous Jew, the most frequent answer isn't Karl Marx or Einstein or Freud or even Rothschild. It's you. That's why your name has become a word in itself. A shylock. What is a shylock? Someone who jews you out of your money. But there must be something more to my inheritance than that. Some reason that, when I see you on stage, I identify with you. Some reason that, when I married my Christian wife, you flashed through my brain and I felt guilty. Or that when an anti-Semitic speaker came onto the campus where I teach, the same image flashed through my head and I felt sick. Some reason that, when I'm watching some stupid daytime talk show with Nazis and skinheads and the KKK, the phrase that goes through my head is "Hath not a Jew eyes." I'm sorry, I know I can't be nearly as eloquent as you are. I never mastered the technique of speaking in verse. But you have. You must have something else to say. Are you a hero or a villain, comic or tragic, a Jew or a gentile? Tell me something new.

SHYLOCK: Here 'tis, most reverend doctor, here it is.

(He removes all but the most basic parts of his costume, putting them back in the casket, which he closes. He delivers the following speech very simply.)

Hath not a Jew eyes? Hath not a Jew hands, organs, dimensions, senses, affections, passions? Fed with the same food, hurt with the same weapons, subject to the same diseases, healed by the same means, warmed and cooled by the same winter and summer as a Christian is?

(SHYLOCK beats his breast, as he did with the "Ashamnu" prayer.)

If you prick us, do we not bleed?

(SHYLOCK beats his breast.)

JACOB: If you prick us, do we not bleed?

(JACOB beats his breast.)

SHYLOCK: If you tickle us, do we not laugh?

(SHYLOCK beats his breast.)

JACOB: If you tickle us, do we not laugh? *(JACOB beats his breast. SHYLOCK softly exits.)* If you poison us, do we not die? *(JACOB beats his breast.)* And if you wrong us, shall we not—no. No. Not me. *(JACOB looks around for SHYLOCK.)* Shylock?

(HAMLET comes out from behind curtain.)

Where's Shylock?

HAMLET: Not again. I thought we just went through all this. Do you want me to help you find him again?

JACOB: No. Never mind. I'd like to go home.

HAMLET: Just click your heels three times...

(HAMLET indicates JACOB's study, which surrounds them.)

JACOB: Yes. Of course.

HAMLET: Jacob?

JACOB: Yes?

HAMLET: Well, we're all waiting. What was he like? Was he a Jew or wasn't he?

JACOB: He was just a character, Hamlet. You need to stop taking him so personally. *(The phone rings.)* Now if you'll excuse me. *(JACOB picks up.)* Hi sweetie. *(Pause)* Sorry, did I sound startled? *(JACOB looks up. HAMLET has gone.)* Not much, just working on that Shylock article. I think I'm getting a little obsessed. It will be good to take a break. *(Pause)* I love you too, Christine. See you soon. Bye.

(Blackout)

One-Eyed Moses and the Churning Red Sea

Original Production

One-Eyed Moses and the Churning Red Sea was presented as part of the Jewish Legends night of Untitled Theater's 24/7 Festival, held at Tada! Theater in New York City in March 2005. The original draft was written and presented within 24 hours, and it was called *Black Moses and the Churning Red Sea.* It was directed by Peter Bloch. Sets were by Alex Senchak, lights by Kevin Hardy. Edward Einhorn was the festival's artistic director, David A. Einhorn was the producer, and Karen Lee Ott was the dramaturg. The cast was as follows:

RABBI TZIPPORAH....................Meredith Kaunitz
MOSES/JOSH ....Skid Maher
MIRIAM/RACHEL ....Alyssa Simon

Not only did the script need to be written between the hours of 10pm and 9am, but all the shows that evening had to adhere to the following rules:

Rule 1: One character must have a Biblical name that is relevant in some way.
Rule 2: The play must involve a dream.
Rule 3: The story must move through time in an unpredictable manner.
Rule 4: The play must include a birth and a death.
Rule 5 (audience suggestion): One of the characters must be a pirate and/or have a hook.

One-Eyed Moses and the Churning Red Sea

A pirate ship, in the middle of the Red Sea. ONE-EYED MOSES, a pirate captain, is calling out to his imaginary shipmates.

MOSES: Argghhh! Avast, ye kvetching knaves, this is what you call sailing? Aye, 'tis a black day when I see such mishegos pass for mastery of the seas.
(MIRIAM, a pirate wench, rushes in.)
MIRIAM: Captain, the Pharaoh is hard aport!
MOSES: A plague on him! Is Aaron manning the cannons?
MIRIAM: Aye, he is.
MOSES: Then fire upon him, and as I be a Semite, we shall part the very waters with our shots.
MIRIAM: The Captain says fire!
(The cannons roar.)
He's still coming, hard astarboard now.
(More cannon fire. The boat rocks.)
We're hit!
MOSES: Great Abraham's balls, who needs this tsurris? Fire again, Aaron, fire again!
(Another shot)
Miriam, we have sailed the seas together a long time now, you and I, and who knows, this voyage may be our last. But to lose to Pharaoh without a fight, that truly would be a shanda. So we shall fight him with all the strength we have

left, and just pray we don't end up in Davy Birnbaum's locker. Fire again, Aaron, fire again!

(There is another cannon shot, and the Pharaoh fires back. MOSES and MIRIAM rush offstage, looking for cover. RABBI TZIPPORAH FINESTEIN enters. She reads from her sermon.)

TZIPPORAH: Moses parted the Red Sea, right? What does that mean? It says in this parsha, "Moses stretched out his hand over the sea; and the Lord drove the sea back by a strong East wind all night, and made the sea dry land, and the waters were divided." Some people think that means there was a low tide, that the Jewish people passed through the water unharmed, but by the time the Egyptians followed, the water had risen. But Rashi points out that it does not say the *water* was divided, it says the *waters* were divided. So he says that not only was the water in the sea divided, but also the water in the cisterns and ditches, not only the terrestrial water, but also the supernatural water. What is supernatural water? In the Midrash Rabbah, it says that when Moses stretched his hand over the waters and commanded it to part, it refused. It said, "Why should I part for you? You were created on the sixth day, but I was created on the third." But then God put God's own hand upon Moses' hand, and the *waters* parted. So I ask again, why are the waters supernatural?

(JOSH and RACHEL, two congregants [played by the actors who played MOSES and MIRIAM], walk up to TZIPPORAH. RACHEL is pregnant.)

JOSH: I enjoyed your sermon, Rabbi. I, uh, got a little lost in the middle. But it was good.

TZIPPORAH: Thank you, Josh. And how are you two doing?

RACHEL: The baby's going to pop out any moment. I think this is the last time I'll be at services, for a few weeks. Until the baby comes.

TZIPPORAH: Mazel Tov. You know, I had the oddest dream, last night, while I was writing this sermon. I dreamt that

Moses was a pirate, and he was fighting the Pharaoh on the high seas. But the two of you were in it, too.

RACHEL: Who were we?

TZIPPORAH: I don't remember.

JOSH: May I speak to you privately, Rabbi?

TZIPPORAH: Of course. What about?

JOSH: Well…

RACHEL: There may be a problem with the baby.

TZIPPORAH: A problem. What sort?

JOSH: They're not sure. Some…irregularities.

TZIPPORAH: Oy. I'm so sorry.

RACHEL: Would you say a mishaberach?

TZIPPORAH: For you, of course.

RACHEL: Not for me. For the baby.

TZIPPORAH: By Jewish law, the baby isn't a person till it's born. That's when it gets its soul. But I could say a personal prayer. When my sister was having a baby, I prayed for it right after the Amidah. There's room for it there.

RACHEL: Thank you, Rabbi.

(They exit. TZIPPORAH is reading the sermon, as before.)

TZIPPORAH: But then God put God's own hand upon Moses' hand, and the *waters* parted. So I ask again, why are the waters supernatural? We know that we need water to live. It is said that when we were in the desert, Miriam, who was a prophetess, was able to find the wells, and without her help, they would not have survived. We ourselves are made from mostly water, as some of you who watch *Star Trek* might remember. Any trekkies out there? I believe some alien in the *Star Trek The Next Generation* referred to us as ugly bags of mostly water. I don't know whether I consider us ugly, but you could think of us, in a way, as animated bags of water…

(TZIPPORAH freezes. ONE-EYED MOSES crawls on, followed by MIRIAM. Oddly, she is pregnant still.)

MOSES: Argghhh, I don't think I'm going to make it.

MIRIAM: Don't give up now. I sense water ahead.

MOSES: Mighty handy, that sense of yours. I wished I'd a known about it before.

MIRIAM: Sensing water on the high seas? I don't know that that's a skill much needed.

MOSES: At least we sent the Pharaoh down to his watery—

MIRIAM: Josh?

MOSES: Nay, me name is One-Eyed Moses...

MIRIAM: My water broke...

MOSES: Aye, 'tis water we seek, my dear.

MIRIAM: No. No. Listen, Josh...

MOSES: I'm not Josh, Mom.

MIRIAM: What?

MOSES: Me name is One-Eyed Moses!

(MOSES and MIRIAM exit. TZIPPORAH resumes talking.)

TZIPPORAH: ...animated bags of water. Animated not only physically, but spiritually, with a spark of God. With a soul. Of course water had to be created first, in order for us to live. Each day God built a building block, so that when he sent his sparks down, they would have something to animate. And when he parted the waters, he parted not only the waters of the Red Sea, he parted the waters within us, as well. For when we left Egypt, we had to leave not only the physical space of Egypt, but also the spiritual space, the space in which we were slaves. We had to learn to be free.

(JOSH enters.)

TZIPPORAH: How is she?

JOSH: She's holding up.

TZIPPORAH: I'm sorry about the baby.

JOSH: Are we supposed to sit shiva, for an infant?

TZIPPORAH: Well, that's partly up to you. Shiva exists for the mourners. Sometimes people choose to sit shiva for a few days in these sorts of instances, but not for the full week. What did you name the child?

JOSH: Moses.

TZIPPORAH: Moshe ben Yahoshua. That's a good name.
JOSH: Thanks.

(JOSH exits and RACHEL enters.)

RACHEL: I had a dream about him, Rabbi.
TZIPPORAH: Really? I've been having some odd dreams myself.
RACHEL: He was all grown up. A man. He had a big beard, and an eye patch over one eye.
TZIPPORAH: An eye patch?
RACHEL: Yes. Well, he, the infant I mean, was born with a problem in his left eye. But in the dream, it was because he was a pirate.
TZIPPORAH: Like in the dream I told you about?
RACHEL: Which dream?
TZIPPORAH: Never mind. Go on. Did he say anything?
RACHEL: Argghhh.
TZIPPORAH: Argghhh?
RACHEL: Yes, but like he really meant it.
TZIPPORAH: How do you really mean argghhh?
RACHEL: I don't know. Like….ARGGHHH!
TZIPPORAH: Uh huh.
RACHEL: What do you think it means?
TZIPPORAH: It sounds like it was just a dream.
RACHEL: No, but, you don't understand. He was speaking. He was trying to say something to me.
TZIPPORAH: What was he trying to say?
RACHEL: I don't know. ARGGHHH!
TZIPPORAH: And what does that mean?
RACHEL: I don't know. I wish I knew.
TZIPPORAH: Maybe it just means that you wish you had gotten to know him, as an adult.
RACHEL: No, no he's speaking. He's saying something.
TZIPPORAH: Arggghh?
RACHEL: No, not like that.

(RACHEL exits. TZIPPORAH goes back to giving her sermon.)

TZIPPORAH: We had to learn to be free. For the first time, when we left Egypt, we had to learn how to be responsible for ourselves. Remember, when we first entered Egypt, we were hardly what you would call a full tribe of people. We were just Jacob and all his descendents. But by the time we left, we were a people. We had an identity. But what was it? We had to find out. When we were slaves we didn't have to know. But now that we were free...

MOSES: Argghhh!

TZIPPORAH: Moses?

MOSES: Argghhh!

TZIPPORAH: She's right, you can be very expressive with that.

MOSES: Arrrr—oh hell, never mind.

TZIPPORAH: What?

MOSES: Nay, ye simply don't understand me.

TZIPPORAH: Understand what?

MOSES: Listen, do you like me best with a patch over my right eye, or my left?

TZIPPORAH: It doesn't really—

MOSES: My right eye was the one with the problem, but I think the left makes me look more manly. What do you think?

TZIPPORAH: Both look...good, I guess.

MOSES: Why didn't ye tell her about the dreams?

TZIPPORAH: What dreams?

MOSES: What dreams? These dreams. Like the one you're having now.

TZIPPORAH: Well, they're just...dreams.

MOSES: So, ye think it's chance that in both your dreams I am One-Eyed Moses, scourge of the Red Sea.

TZIPPORAH: I guess.

MOSES: Ye be a wise lass, but sometimes ye make as much sense as me cabin boy, Meshugenah Jack.

TZIPPORAH: So it's not a coincidence?

MOSES: Have you heard of a gilgul?

TZIPPORAH: Is that some sort of pirate thing?

MOSES: Some pirate thing? It's a Hebrew word.

TZIPPORAH: Oh. *(Pause)* What does it mean?

MOSES: You're a rabbi. Aren't you supposed to know this stuff?

TZIPPORAH: I could look it up.

MOSES: It's a soul that enters a new body when a child is born.

TZIPPORAH: Ah. It's a legend from the Kabala. I don't really believe in those legends.

MOSES: Well believe in it or not, that's what I be. And I'm afraid you're stuck with me.

TZIPPORAH: Stuck with you? How come?

MOSES: Because me last body was nothing more than an ugly bag of mostly water.

TZIPPORAH: Argghhh.

MOSES: That's what I said.

(MOSES exits. TZIPPORAH is reading her sermon again.)

TZIPPORAH: Now that we were free we had to learn who we were. Our souls were parted, they were opened by God, but he asked us to wander the desert for forty years afterwards. It was forty years till we learned. There is one last story I would like to share with you. When the waters were parted, it is said, they wouldn't fully part until one man actually put his toe in and stepped forward. In order to learn what it was like to be free, he had to have the courage to take the first step.

(RACHEL enters. TZIPPORAH seems ill.)

RACHEL: What's wrong?

TZIPPORAH: I've been sick every morning when I get up.

RACHEL: For how long?

TZIPPORAH: Ever since... For a while.

RACHEL: I know how that feels. From when I was pregnant. But I have been feeling much better, this time.

TZIPPORAH: This time?

RACHEL: I'm pregnant!
TZIPPORAH: You are?
RACHEL: Yes.
TZIPPORAH: Thank God. I mean Mazel Tov. It sounds like a good decision. For the two of you, I mean.
RACHEL: Thank you.
TZIPPORAH: How long till you have the baby?
RACHEL: Six months.
TZIPPORAH: Oy. Well, I think I can last that long.
RACHEL: *You* can last that long?
TZIPPORAH: I love babies.
RACHEL: Me too.
TZIPPORAH: Are you having those pirate dreams anymore?
RACHEL: What pirate dreams?
TZIPPORAH: Nothing. Never mind.
RACHEL: *(Jokingly)* Argghhh!
TZIPPORAH: Same to you. To both of you.

APPENDIX:
Facts About the Characters

APPENDIX:

Facts About the Characters

The Golem

Golem originally meant, depending on the source, "embryo" or "imperfect matter," though now it is a Hebrew and Yiddish slang term for a thick-skulled person. Stories of a creature of clay by that name appear as early as the twelfth century. In the *Sefer Gezirah,* published at that time in Worms, Poland, it states that in a magic ritual, gestures are as important as numbers (or letters) in the Golem's creation. In the sixteenth century, an early golem was credited to Rabbi Elijah Ball Shem of Chelm.

The modern stories of the Golem are many. In almost all of them, the Golem is summoned in response to Christian attacks precipitated by the blood libel, the once commonly held belief that the blood of Christian children was a main ingredient of matzo. In almost all of them, the Golem goes out of control and the Maharal must turn him back into clay. A number of smaller stories have also cropped up along with the main legend. Among the best known is the story of how the Golem was asked by the Rebbetsin to get water, despite warnings from the Maharal not to use him as a servant. The incident nearly ends in disaster, for she forgets to tell the Golem when to stop, resulting in a near flood (a somewhat similar misadventure would later be enacted by Mickey Mouse in "The Sorcerer's Apprentice" section of *Fantasia*).

In some legends, the Golem is animated by something written on his forehead, in some a paper placed under his tongue, and in some an amulet. The fact that the Golem is named Joseph and the idea that it is half demon also commonly occurs within the legends. However, Joseph's earlier relationship with the Maharal's daughter is purely an invention of the adaptation.

Perhaps the most famous adaptations of the Golem legend are the play by Yiddish playwright H. Levick; the German expressionist silent film written and directed by Henrik Galeen and Paul Wegener; the book by Isaac Bashevis Singer; and Michael Chambon's recent incorporation of the legend into his book *Kavalier and Clay.* Of course, many similar creatures to the Golem, perhaps inspired by the Jewish legend, have popped up in literature, ranging from the Monster in *Frankenstein* to The Incredible Hulk (originally, the Hulk's skin was gray, like clay, rather than the later green coloring).

The Golem is supposedly locked in the attic of the Alteschul, the ancient synagogue which still stands in Prague. In recent years, a journalist went into the attic to investigate, but he found nothing.

The Maharal (Rabbi Judah Loew ben Bezalel)

There are disputes as to when and where the Rabbi Loew was born—possibly in Posen, Poland in 1512, possibly in Worms in 1520. Regardless, after studying and becoming a rabbi in a Polish yeshiva, he came to Prague to marry his wife, Pearla, in 1544. She was 28 at the time. Afterwards, he became Chief Rabbi for the Moravian Jews, until 1573, when he returned to Prague.

Rabbi Loew was a distinguished scholar and an expert on the Kabala, and his reputation earned him the nickname the Maharal (a Hebrew abbreviation that stands for "Our Teacher, Rabbi Loew"). He was also a prolific writer and some of his writing was a forerunner to Hasidic thought. Rabbi Loew was conservative in his approach to Judaism, decrying the drinking of unkosher wine in the community and declaring that the Talmud should not be taught to the young, only those who are intellectually ready. He also did not believe that advances in science had any relevance to the interpretation of the Torah.

The story of the Golem didn't become attached to Rabbi Loew until the 1800's, the first published record of it being in 1838, by the German Czech journalist Franz Klutschack, though he was recording an already existing legend. Many other miraculous stories have accumulated about the Rabbi as well, and the Hasidim consider him a Zaddik, a holy man whose connection with God allowed him to perform many miracles.

Rabbi Loew died on August 17, 1609 and was buried in the Old Jewish Cemetery in Prague, where his gravestone still gathers much attention.

Methuselah

This is what it says in Genesis about Methuselah: "When Methuselah had lived 187 years, he became the father of Lamech. Methuselah lived after the birth of Lamech 782 years, and had other sons and daughters. Thus all the days of Methuselah were 969 years, and he died."

Those 969 years are more than any other person in the Torah is credited with, but considering that fact, Methuselah has very few stories or legends associated with him. Interestingly, he is the oldest by only a few years—his grandfather Jared is credited with 962 years and his grandson Noah is credited with 950 years. Quick calculation can discover that the year of Methuselah's death coincides with the year of the Flood—at which time, one would guess, he died with the rest of the sinners. Or, according to the play, lived on, to sin some more…

Pearla (Rebbetsin Loew)

Pearla was the daughter of Reb Samuel Schmelke Reich, a rich merchant, and she became engaged to the future Rabbi

Loew at a very young age. However, her father reportedly lost his fortune and was unable to pay her dowry, as promised. Rather than abandon Pearla, Rabbi Loew waited for their fortunes to improve, and, the legend goes, Pearla's fortunes were restored when she found a bag of gold mistakenly thrown at her by a soldier. The legend further states that the soldier was the Prophet Elijah in disguise.

Pearla worked for many years at a bakery shop and later at the synagogue as an accountant, a job common among many of the women in the Jewish community. Together, she and Rabbi Loew had six daughters and a son. Pearla died in 1619, ten years after Rabbi Loew, and was buried at his side.

Rivka and Devorah (the Rabbi's children)

Rabbi Loew and his wife Pearla had six daughters, who were, from oldest to youngest, Leah, Feigeleh, Gitteleh, Reichel, Tillah, and Realina. They also had a son, Bezalel, who was killed during a pogrom in Germany. He was serving as a rabbi there at the time. All of Rabbi Loew's daughters married Rabbis, as well. Chronologically, Tillah would have fit Devorah's role and Realina would fit Rivka, though their similarities end there. Realina, in fact, reportedly married Rabbi Loew's brother, Rabbi Chaim, the Chief Rabbi of Worms.

Rudolf II

The Emperor Rudolf II of Austria (1552-1612) was born on July 18, 1552 as the eldest son of Maximilian II. He became King of Bohemia in 1575 and was made Emperor in 1576. In 1583, he moved the imperial court to Prague and proceeded to transform Prague into a city filled with astronomers, alchemists, artists, craftsmen, and humanists. He was fascinated with any sort of new knowledge, whether it was in science or the occult. He gathered an enormous collection of art, including (among many others) the works of Bosch and

Arcimboldo, and filled the castle with a menagerie of exotic animals. His longtime lover, Anna Maria Strada, daughter of Ottavio Strada, the Court Painter, bore him numerous illegitimate children. The oldest of them, Julius Caesar, notoriously murdered his mistress in 1608. Emperor Rudolf was also rumored to have many other lovers, some of them men.

It is known that Emperor Rudolf met with Rabbi Loew at the palace, though the full details of that meeting are not known. Rumors and reconstructions of that meeting have been many, usually focusing on Rudolf's interest in the mystical and Rabbi Loew's familiarity with the Kabala. The Rabbi's knowledge of the ancient texts was extensive and sometimes quite different from prevailing opinions, especially in his interpretation of the Sephirot, the ten aspects of God. There are also rumors of other, unrecorded meetings. Emperor Rudolf's relationship with the Jewish community was positive on the whole—he changed the laws to allow Jews fair trials and removed restrictions on trade. However, he still required them to wear the yellow circle that was the mark of Judaism in Prague at the time.

As Emperor Rudolf grew older, he suffered increasingly from the mood swings that had plagued him somewhat in his younger days, becoming more depressive and reclusive. In 1611, Rudolf's brother, heir, and longtime rival, Matthias, used those depressive spells and fears of a Protestant takeover as an excuse to march on Prague Castle. Matthias forced Rudolf to turn over the rulership of Hungary, Moravia, and Bohemia, although Rudolf kept the Imperial Crown and his residence in the castle. Emperor Rudolf died on January 19, 1612.

Serach

There are three mentions of Serach in the Torah. The first is in Genesis, in a passage that begins "These are the names of the Israelites, Jacob and his descendants, who came to

Egypt," and continues to mention all of Jacob's sons, his daughter Dinah, his grandsons, and one granddaughter—Serach. The passage reads "The sons of Asher: Imnah, Ishvah, Ishvi, Beri'ah, with Serach their sister." This sentence is repeated in Chronicles. One would suppose that, since the Torah mentions 53 grandsons and only one granddaughter, she was a person of significance.

The second time Serach is mentioned is in Numbers, in the listing of Israelites who escaped from Egypt, where it simply says "And the name of the daughter of Asher was Serach."

Since Serach is mentioned both as Jacob's granddaughter and also as one of the people who escaped from Egypt over 400 years later, Serach is often referred to as the oldest woman in the Torah. A number of midrashim (stories based on the Torah) have been written about her.

The most well known of those midrashim tells of how she plays a harp for Jacob, gently mixing in the words that his son Joseph is "alive and the ruler of all Egypt," so that the news does not come as too much of a shock for him. In return, Jacob blesses her, saying "May you live forever and never die." According to that story, she never does, eventually entering Paradise alive.

There are also stories of her identifying Moses as the man who will lead the Israelites to freedom, and of her telling Moses where to find where Jacob was buried, although his body had been placed in a lead casket on the bottom of the Nile river when he died. Some consider her the guardian of Israel's communal memory.

Shylock

Shylock is, of course, the famous Jew from Shakespeare's *The Merchant of Venice.* He follows in the tradition of Barabas from Marlowe's *The Jew of Malta,* an extremely villainous caricature who says of himself "I...kill sick people groaning under walls: Sometimes I go about and poison wells." Jews were stock villains of the time, with stock vices: avarice, gross features, and a sort of scheming cleverness—much like the Ferengi of the modern day Star Trek series, with, in the Elizabethan's mind, as little reality.

For a while after its initial performances, *The Merchant of Venice* disappeared from the stage, reappearing in adaptation in George Granville's *The Jew of Venice* as a purely comic character. However, the actor Charles Macklin brought the original Shylock back, in a tragic though equally villainous interpretation. During the next hundred years or so, a number of notable portrayals of the character in the same vein followed, by actors such as Edmund Kean and William Charles Macready.

The first sympathetic Shylock came in the late 1800's, as interpreted by Henry Irving. After that, many more sympathetic Shylocks followed, though for a long time they were the exception more than the rule. These stage interpretations were divided between the old villain and the put upon and more justifiably angry representation more common today.

Other shades of Shylock cropped up over time, as Freudian interpretations and Marxist interpretations became more popular. The Freudians concentrated on his relationship with his daughter above all (though Freud himself was more concerned with Portia and Bassanio), and the Marxists were more interested in Shylock as a typical capitalist.

In the Nazi era, Shylock became an anti-Semitic icon, and the play was loved by Hitler. But afterwards it became difficult to portray him in that manner, and it is unusual to see a production nowadays that doesn't try an at least somewhat sympathetic portrayal.

Thaddeus

There is no evidence of a historical figure that corresponds to Thaddeus, though he is found in most versions of the

Golem legend. However, it is true that the Bohemian Jesuits in particular were very anti-Semitic at that time and that many of the priests perpetuated the blood libel. Thaddeus is probably just a compilation of a number of real-life figures.

Bibliography

These are some of the fascinating books I consulted while writing these plays and the appendix. Unfortunately, this is only a partial list, since I did much of my research years ago and left many of the books, forgotten, on library reference shelves.

Ausubel, Nathan. *A Treasury of Jewish Folklore.* New York: Crown Publishers, 1948.

Bialik, Haayim Nahman and Yehoshua Hana Ravnitzky, eds. *Book of Legends/Sefer Ha-Aggadah: Legends from the Talmud and Midrash.* Translated by William G. Braude. New York: Schnocken, 1992.

Demetz, Peter. *Prague in Black and Gold.* New York: Hill and Wang, 1997.

Evans, R. J. W. *Rudolf II and His World.* Oxford: Thames and Hudson, 1997 (Orig ed. 1973.)

Gross, John. *Shylock: A Legend and Its Legacy.* New York: Touchstone, 1992.

Hammer, Jill. *Sisters at Sinai: New Tales of Biblical Women.* Philadelphia: Jewish Publication Society of America, 2001.

Maresova, Sona, trans. *The Prague Golem: Jewish Stories of the Ghetto.* Prague: Vitalis, 2002.

Schulman, Yaakov David. *The Maharal of Prague: The Story of Yehudah Loew.* New York, London, Jerusalem: CIS Publishers, 1992.

Seifert, Lucy. *The Mysterious Golem.* Translated by Anna Bryson Gustova. Prague: Petr Prchal, 2004.

Shapiro, James. *Shakespeare and the Jews.* New York: Columbia University Press, 1996.

Acknowledgements:

Thank you to everyone who helped throughout the editing process and the play readings which accompanied it:

Delia Baseman, Peter Bean, Glory Sims Bowen, Jennifer Chudy, David A. Einhorn, Saysha Heinzman, Robert Honeywell, Talaura Harms, Ian W. Hill, Uma Incrocci, Berit Johnson, Kathryn Velvel Jones, Tanya Khordoc, Skid Maher, David Maxine, Jesse May, Celia Montgomery, Meredith Kaunitz, Nancy Nagrant, Grant Neale, Karen Ott, Andrew Rothkin, Eric Shanower, Ken Simon, Richard Simon, Jennifer Stokes, Tziona Szajman, Emy Zener, and Maxwell Zener

Printed in the United States
42985LVS00002B/63